SELF PROTECTION

SELF-PROTECTION

THE ART OF PREVENTATIVE SELF-DEFENSE

DAVID J. MATHENA

Copyright © 2014 by David J. Mathena

All rights reserved. This book or any portion thereof may not be reproduced or used in any manner whatsoever without the express written permission of the publisher except for the use of brief quotations in a book review.

ISBN: 978-1-312-27608-6

The publisher has used its best endeavors to ensure that the URLs for external websites referred to in this book are correct and active at the time of going to press. However, the publisher and the author have no responsibility for the websites and can make no guarantee that a site will remain live or that the content will remain relevant, decent or appropriate.

First Edition

Typesetting by wordzworth.com

This book is dedicated to the late
H. "Billy" L. Putnam and his family.

CONTENTS

Preface		i
About the Author		iii
Introduction		v
Lesson 1	Protective Concepts	1
Lesson 2	The ADD/RAG Process	5
	Avoid Threats	6
	Deter Threats from Attacking You	11
	Detect/Identify Threats	16
	Respond to Attacks	19
	Assess Incidents to learn from the Experience	22
	Going Forward; Applying Lessons Learned	25
Lesson 3	Emergency planning and Practice	29
Lesson 4	Self-defense Basics	33
	Fight Physiology	37
	Principles of Self Defense	47
Lesson 5	Weapons	69
	Firearms	70
	Knives	80
	Sticks	84
Conclusion		89

PREFACE

I was born in the Meridian, Mississippi of 1979. It was a different city from the one we see today. It wasn't Atlanta or New York; it had a small town feel to it. The neighborhood in which I lived with my grandmother and great-grandmother was quiet and well kept. Our next door neighbors, the Johnsons were nice, cordial folks who worked hard and stayed out of trouble. Mr. Johnson even mowed my grandmother's lawn until I was old enough to do so. It wasn't unusual to see people helping each other when the need arose.

Growing up I walked to Marion Park Elementary School from my grandmother's house on 25th Avenue, and nobody ever questioned my safety. My parents and I later moved to the North Hills area of Meridian, and I walked to North West Junior High every weekday. I spent one Saturday a month walking North Hills Street alone with my cash allowance, trudging from the bowling alley, to the skating rink, to Indy's right beside McDonald's, and then to a friend's house almost three miles away on Highway 493 to spend the rest of the weekend playing video games. There were rules to follow, and for the most part I followed them: be indoors by dark, never disrespect an adult, and look both ways before crossing the street. But I don't believe my safety was ever in question. In my early twenties I walked the same portion of North Hills Street to work at various fast food restaurants, still never fearing for my safety.

When I went to work for the Lauderdale County Detention Facility in 2002, I was oblivious to the crime we had in Meridian. I knew that people used drugs; I saw that fairly regularly. I saw people driving after having too much to drink, and I heard about so-and-so beating his wife again. I even had a bicycle stolen from me once, in my grandmother's neighborhood. But I honestly thought that my rustic little home town was devoid of "serious" criminals like murderers, rapists, and robbers. It surprised me to see how many people were being charged with those sorts of crimes, and it was then that I realized that Meridian wasn't that small anymore.

Fast forward to present day Meridian. On Mother's Day of this year, Billy Putnam, an 87-year old Navy veteran was deliberately shot and killed in an armed robbery on North Hills Street – the same street I once spent my childhood weekend recreation, and the same street where I walked to work in my early adulthood. This was just one of many reports of various shootings, robberies, rapes, and gang-related offenses that have saturated the news and social media posts this year. But this heinous murder sparked an outrage in the community, and it ignited the inspiration in me to write this book for the people – the would-be victims of Meridian, Mississippi, and for those who don't call Meridian home. It is my sincerest hope that this book will make a difference, that it will help someone to avoid being the victim of a crime like the murder of Billy Putnam and others who have senselessly lost their lives or their peace of mind. May the peace of God rest upon us all.

– David J. Mathena

ABOUT THE AUTHOR

David J. Mathena is a freelance author, security consultant and self-defense expert. He has over 15 years of commercial and industrial security experience, and over 17 years martial arts and self-defense training & experience. David has been teaching martial arts and self-defense for over a decade and has multiple instructor-level certifications.

INTRODUCTION

"The police won't come in here," the thug said, crossing his arms in defiance. The security officer had just called the police for the third time to get help with what seemed an impossible task – clearing the streets at curfew time at DeVille Apartments in Dekalb, Mississippi. It had been two years since a security guard had attempted to enforce the rules in DeVille. All six companies before this one had failed to secure the low-income apartment complex, and the manager had given up on hiring guards. While it was a camera system that Robin wanted, a good security team is what she needed the most.

I sent one officer the first night, an experienced bouncer who I knew could take care of himself if the need arose. The next day my officer reported back to me.

"One man can't do this job," he said. There had been fight upon fight, and the police refused to respond to the officer's many requests for assistance.

For the next two weeks I sent two officers instead of one, and I came also, tripling the show of force at Deville. It was a dangerous job; we were representatives of authority in an unending block party of drugs, alcohol, and violence. I received plenty of advice from people who understood only conventional wisdom; I heard statements like, "you've got to put your foot down and show 'em you mean business.", and "demand respect; if you let them disrespect you they'll run all over you." I was told that "these people" only respond to handcuffs and jail cells. But I knew better. I'd worked this kind of detail before. "These people" were just like any other; they wanted to feel safe, they wanted to be respected, and they wanted to be heard when they felt wronged. I personally trained my officers to take a customer service approach, giving respect and serving others above demanding respect for their positions of authority. I also collaborated with the Chief of the Kemper County Sheriff's Department, without whose help we never would accomplish much more than the previous six companies.

The remainder of that weekend and the next week we spoke with tenants and assured them that we were not there to take over their homes, but to protect them. We enforced rules that had not previously been acknowledged, explaining that those rules are what would keep them and their families safe. Once we got compliance from the residents, we found that the majority of problems stemmed from unwanted visitors, so we began to control access to the property. We gained control of the property and brought peace to Deville Apartments in just two weeks, a feat that six other companies had not been able to do in all the years that they had been given.

In this book you will find a wealth of knowledge concerning security and self-protection, most of which comes from my own experiences as a security officer, self-defense instructor, small business owner, and security consultant. As an individual and previous owner of a small business, I understand the concept of affordability; I know that most people aren't wealthy enough to afford bodyguards and expensive camera and alarm systems for their homes. I know that small businesses need to maximize their profits in order to succeed, which means not spending a lot of money on security systems and teams. I also have a heart for the protection of life and a mind for the protection of property, and I have become known for my expertise in developing solutions to complicated problems concerning facility security in an affordable way. It doesn't take expensive cameras, biometric devices, and access control systems to secure yourself, your home, and your family. It just takes ingenuity and "want-to".

In the decade or so that I have taught self-defense, I developed a very simple system of my own, borrowing from many of the other systems and martial arts styles already in existence. But before I would teach someone self-defense I almost always outlined some methods which the student could use to avoid having to fight. I never wanted my teachings to have to be used; I'd much rather the students live peaceably knowing that if they ever needed the skills, they would have them. Over time I refined the system and gave it a name: The Victor System (as in, "to the victor go the spoils").

The Victor System is not a commercialized self-defense system which promises to make you a semi-professional mixed martial arts fighter capable of destroying your opponent with secret techniques practiced by Kung Fu Ninjas in an ancient monastery somewhere in the mountains of Asia (not that there's anything wrong with Kung Fu Ninjas...). Instead, the Victor System employs methods used by executive protection agents and security specialists to *prevent* loss events from occurring to their clients, thereby reducing the damage a hundred fold.

Think about it: Every fight is different because every person is different, and each fight incorporates two different individual person's sets of variables. Add a third set of variables – the outside variables; the ones caused by the weather, time of day, the setting in which the fight takes place, bystanders and accomplices, and so on. Even a well-trained soldier with intimate knowledge of combat can only hope to control some of these variables, and as such can only expect about a 25-40% increase by improving his own variables! Would you rather respond to an attack with a 25-40% chance of surviving, or prevent the attack with a solid 100% chance of surviving? I'd personally rather increase my chances of surviving, thank you. With the Victor System the odds in your favor of surviving a human threat increase exponentially. No commercially available self-defense system on earth can truthfully give you such a claim.

THE GOAL OF THE VICTOR SYSTEM

In order to be successful at anything, we must first define success. What is it that you wish to accomplish? What are the terms and conditions that will indicate that you have succeeded? The goal of any victim at the time of his or her attack is to survive the worst moment of their life up to that point. Period. I won't pull out the smoke and mirrors in an attempt to make you believe the impossible claims you will find on many self-defense websites. You know the ones: "Our self-defense system is called the most devastatingly powerful, scientifically proven self-defense system in the world today." "Learn the world's most dangerous fighting secrets!" These claims are what I call "commercial fluff". Aimed at the gullible and inexperienced consumer, these "instructors" victimize their customers by taking their money in return for a class, a book, some DVD's, and "free" advice via a periodic newsletter – material that can get a new fighter killed if they were to try to apply it against someone who has an aggressive, predatory mindset. Sure, some of the commercially available defensive tactics systems are good. But what they all seem to be devoid of is how not to get yourself into the predicament in which you must use their system in the first place! When, in fact, it is that avoidance mindset that is most effective at protecting one's self in the real world. That is what this book is specifically designed to do.

So let me be clear: **the goal of the Victor System is to assist you in avoiding threats, thereby empowering you to survive.** Keep this in mind while reading. The goal is not to teach you how to fight, win, or even finish the fight, but to avoid, prevent, and deter the fight from ever happening.

That being said, this particular volume does contain some principles of self-defense that I have personally found very useful in my many years of martial arts and self-defense training and experience. Just in case you find it impossible to prevent being caught up in a violent situation, this knowledge could save your life. But please do not mistake the purpose of this system; *an ounce of prevention is worth a pound of cure.*

LESSON 1

PROTECTIVE CONCEPTS

Before you can effectively defend yourself from any threat, it will benefit you to understand the concepts of vulnerability, threat, and attack. So, here goes:

A vulnerability

Is a **weakness in your defense** which leaves you susceptible to attack. Everyone has vulnerabilities. It is impossible to cover every base. Even a full detail of presidential Secret Service agents can't protect their clients from everything. They can only mitigate (lessen) the risk of attacks by reducing vulnerabilities. An example of a vulnerability is being unaware of your surroundings. By not being aware of what is around you, you can miss obvious cues which would otherwise alert you to danger.

A threat

For the purposes of this system, is a **person who has expressed a potential** for an attack. While in many self-defense systems there are different levels of awareness which correspond to various levels of threats, in the Victor System there are just two types of threats: those that originate inside your social circle, and those that come from without. Anyone who has expressed the intent to cause harm to you or anyone around you is considered a threat. An example of an internal threat would be allowing a sexual predator in your home (the predator is the threat; your unawareness of his personality is a vulnerability). An external threat may be the loss of personal information over the Internet (the person or persons taking the information is the threat; your ignorance concerning information security is a vulnerability). The difference between internal and external threats is your acquaintance and relationship with the threat. If you know the person who threatens you; if you allow that person access to your life, your home, your information, or your family, then that person is considered to be inside your social circle – he or she is an internal threat. Conversely, if you do not know the attacker, or if you no longer associate with the person, then he is an external threat.

An attack

Is an **action taken** which has a high probability of causing a "loss event" (death, injury, loss of personal information, money or valuables, reputation, or family environment). An attack is always caused by a threat, whether known or unknown. In the case of the sexual predator, the attack does not occur until the predator takes action to molest or rape a victim. The loss of information is not necessarily an attack in and of itself, but the use of that information is. As you can see, not all attacks are physical; some are proprietary, reputational, or environmental. The differences are discussed below.

A physical attack

Is just as it sounds: an attack which can cause physical harm to someone. Whether it is a mugger on the street, an assault in a nightclub or the rape of yourself or a family member, a physical attack can be the most instantaneously devastating event to happen to someone.

A proprietary attack

Is an attack on a person's or a family's property. This includes anything that is owned – money, financial information, home, vehicle, etc. A proprietary attack can be in the form of theft, loss of an item, its use or its value, vandalism or destruction, and can leave a person feeling "raped" or infiltrated long after the attack has passed, especially if the attack occurs at the person's home.

A reputational attack

Occurs whenever a person's reputation in the family, community, or social circle is tainted. This can be the result of slander or libel, where slander is the unwritten manufacture of (usually false) statements which harm someone's reputation, and libel is the written defamation of one's character. A reputational attack can also manifest in the form of an event which causes the victim's reputation to be devalued, such as being accused or convicted of an immoral act. Unfortunately, many reputational attacks are initiated internally, by friends of friends, coworkers, classmates, and the like. It can be difficult to find a solution to reputational attacks, specifically in personal circles, because much of society labels those who respond with anything less than acceptance as being overly sensitive, thin skinned or just plain weak. But don't be fooled; these are very real attacks that can cause very real psychological damage.

An environmental attack

Can be anything that damages the family or social environment – bullying, whether online or in person, is a prime example of an environmental attack. So are child abuse and domestic violence. Like a reputational attack, this kind of attack most often comes from within the social circle, such as a parent, spouse, or supposed friend. Because of the emotional proximity of the attacker to the victim, some people find it difficult to properly deal with or respond to these attacks. It can be difficult for people to stop their children, spouses, or coworkers from hurting them, because ironically they do not want to damage the emotional environment. It can be especially hard for children to take any action against their parents, because they may not know that they have options. However, it is imperative that action is taken to stop the attack.

Many attacks can take on the characteristics of more than one type of attack. The brutal rape of a female member of a family, for instance is obviously a physical attack, but the reputation of the girl may be called into question by extremely conservative members of the community (imagine people making statements like, "What was she doing on that side of town? Why was she wearing that dress? I heard she was sexually active anyway."), and the girl's emotional state after the trauma of being sexually assaulted, perhaps by someone she knew and trusted, can leave the entire family at odds with each other, taking on the characteristics of an environmental attack.

What do all of these attacks have in common? All of them cause a loss event - death, injury, personal information, money or valuables, reputation, or social environment; all of them are caused by threats, whether internal or external; and most importantly, all of them can be prevented! The next section discusses specific steps which can be taken to avoid facing a devastating loss event, and some examples of real life incidents which have contributed to the knowledge that these steps actually do work.

LESSON 2

THE ADD/RAG PROCESS

As stated before, the Victor System is focused mainly on crime prevention, rather than response to it. While most self-defense systems teach students how to respond to attacks, The Victor System encourages you to address vulnerabilities and threats. However, you must remain ready to defend yourself should the need arise. In order to do this, we use a method that many security specialists and executive protection agents alike use to prevent crimes against their clients. That process is something akin to what I call the "ADD/RAG" process. While the professionals use a much more complicated and in-depth process, I have simplified it for personal use. I use this myself, and it has been phenomenal at keeping me out of harm's way, and it is the system I recommend to anyone who has been a victim of any sort of attack.

The following steps can be used anywhere for groups of any size against threats and vulnerabilities of all sorts. As you can see, the first letters make up the acronym **ADD/RAG**. Notice the "back-slash" (/) between the D and the R. That denotes a shift in thinking, from avoidance to response to an imminent attack.

Here are the specific steps in the ADD/RAG Process:

Avoid threats

Deter threats from attacking you

Detect/Identify threats

Respond to attacks

Assess incidents to learn from the experience

Going Forward; applying lessons learned

AVOID THREATS

As we have already established, avoidance is the name of the game. Avoiding a bad situation is much better than having to respond to it. But first you must know what you are trying to avoid. While I could get very technical (as if I haven't already!), I will simplify things and say that you should primarily avoid dangerous people.

Who is dangerous? Here is a good standard to live by; if a person has been known to engage in criminal or immoral acts, or regularly associates with people who do, avoid them! Notice that I said, "*known* to engage in criminal/immoral acts". That doesn't mean you have to wait until they are confronted, arrested or convicted. If you know that the person is doing bad things, keep away from them! If you see someone hanging out with people who give you the impression of being troublemakers, don't let him or his criminal friends come into your life and steal from you or hurt you. If you suspect they may be involved with immoral activities, it is better to shy away and be wrong, than chance it and be right. Many people have been killed by folks they wanted so badly to trust, even though their instincts told them not to.

One way you can find out if someone you don't know well is a dangerous person is to do some basic investigating. Talk to people who know the person. Listen if they tell you he is abusive, controlling, if he's a cheater, or is a drug user or alcoholic. Take heed when they say someone has anger issues. These red flags should tell you clearly to avoid the person, especially if you hear it from more than one source.

If someone you want to know more about has a Facebook account or other social media channel, check it out. People put all sorts of information on social media websites, and you can find out a lot about someone's personality just by reading his or her daily posts. Pay special attention to the language the person uses. If a person complains too much, speaks negatively day after day, or makes comments about hurting other people or himself, these can be viewed as warning signs. Also, take a look at the photographs; there should be pictures of other people or things that makes the person happy, like cars, flowers, or animals. If the photo album is slam full of "selfies" (pictures of the person he took of himself), there's a good chance that this person is very self-centered and you will need to probe farther to be sure you don't miss any other underlying character flaws. Selfishness is the number one cause of crime, sin, divorce, and heartbreak in the world. Fact, not opinion.

Perform a background check to find out more about the person's past. For a nominal fee, you can go to a website like *www.intelius.com* and find a lot of information on a person. In order to save money, I suggest you only use this option on people you are considering dating or having a close personal or business relationship with. Also, for free you can check the national sex offender registry. This is an absolute must if the person you are considering befriending is to be around your children at all. Do the homework before you get to know the person intimately, because it can be very difficult to make a rational decision once your emotions are involved.

Although performing a criminal history check on someone can reveal secrets about their past, there are millions of people who have not been caught or convicted for their wrongdoings. For this purpose, I have listed some characteristics of people you should steer clear of. If someone you know displays two or more of these behaviors, you should regard it as a big, waving red flag and take appropriate action to ensure the safety of yourself and your family.

What to look out for in dangerous people:

- Lack of empathy for others; doesn't seem to care about other people's welfare or feelings
- Selfishness – puts his or her wants and needs above everyone else's
- Hostile masculinity; Macho/aggressive and dominant or controlling personality
- Emotional constriction
- Demeaning or belittling; puts others down
- Making statements like, "Nobody will ever love you like I do"
- Hostile and threatening; very angry personality, prone to bully or start fights or arguments
- Has extreme mood swings – could be described by some as "bipolar"
- Substance abuse (excessive alcohol; illegal drugs; abuse of prescription drugs)
- Contempt for authority; openly disregards laws and rules
- Ignoring social, emotional, or physical boundaries or limits
- Using teasing or belittling language to keep someone from setting his or her own standards or limits
- Does not allow others to maintain friendships or normal relationships with friends or family
- Talks about hurting people, killing others or self.
- Physical violence; striking, grabbing, shoving, thumping, punching others.
- Punching doors or walls, breaking objects out of anger.
- Screaming uncontrollably at a person, object, or incident (anger issues)

Now that you have a good idea of what to avoid, it is up to you to look for these signs in people. If you see character traits which may suggest they can be criminal or abusive, stay away! Additionally, if you just have a bad feeling or premonition about someone, trust your instincts. Don't wait until you find out why you feel this way; avoid the person now!

Avoidance has a lot to do with trust. How much access to your life you allow someone should depend a lot on how much trust he or she has earned. Imagine that you own a bank. You control the building and everything that happens within its walls. You are responsible for the bank's resources, the actions of the bank, and what happens to it. That bank represents your life. It's your home. It's your family. You deal with people every day, and you must have a system in place which dictates how much trust you allow certain people, because if you don't, those people will take advantage of you and your family, and attacks will flood in from as many sources as you allow. There are four levels of trust that the Victor System recognizes for personal use. These four levels of trust are not to be confused with the designation of internal and external threats, but they work in conjunction with those designations.

1. **Outsiders**: The vast majority of people in the world belong in this circle. At this level, the person has either not earned your trust, or has actually betrayed it. The best way to describe them is to say you don't trust them at all. Your cheating ex will fit nicely in this circle. Any threat that exists externally will come from this group.

2. **Acquaintances**: People you know slightly. If you have just met someone, or have known them for twenty years, but have had no daily interaction on a personal level with that person, he is an acquaintance. While you may feel like you've known your coworker forever, if you haven't actually associated with him outside the office, you only know his "public

face", and he should only be trusted at this level. Acquaintances should only be afforded a little trust, because they have not had the honor of earning your trust yet. Likewise, they have not been given the opportunity to betray it – are you getting the picture yet?

3   **Friends:** While society has accepted the use of the word "friend" to include hundreds of people we barely know in passing, we aren't that naïve. We call it like it is – a friend is someone who has earned your trust over time. You've spent time at their house, they've visited yours also, and you know that most of their values, ideals, and morals are similar to your own. You know enough about them to make an *informed* decision to call this person a "real/true friend", and they have not betrayed your trust in any way in at least a year of knowing them.

4   **Inner Circle:** Your Inner Circle of Trust is filled with a select few individuals who have earned your highest level of trust over many years of personal interaction with them. They are not your closest friends because you have a lot of fun with them – although you may have a blast with them, that's not the point. They are your most trusted because they have earned their way into that position by helping you when you needed it, supporting you emotionally when you were vulnerable, and most of all, never betraying your trust! Your Inner Circle of Trust may contain your spouse, your parents, or one or two friends who you can safely predict will never be disloyal to you. Or perhaps you have not found anyone who fits that description. It's better to be honest with yourself and know that you have some friends, but none you can truly trust, than to fool yourself into becoming a victim.

A word about trust: trust is a valuable thing. Too often I see people freely handing out their trust to unworthy people, and then they end up getting hurt, abused, and victimized by the people they placed their trust in. And after a few times of misplacing trust in the wrong people, many put up emotional walls and find it hard to have faith in anyone at all. In short, they lurch from one extreme to another; they trust implicitly until they are tired of being hurt, at which time they stop trusting altogether. While not trusting anyone ever can be a more secure way of living, it is also a very lonely, unpleasant way of life. I would not wish it upon anyone. If you have not already erected those walls, take my advice regarding trust: Trust should be earned over time. Give people a crumb of trust and let them earn the rest. If they are faithful with a little trust for a while, then give them a little more. Allow them to earn your confidence over time until you have no reason to believe they mean you any harm. And if they abuse the faith you have given them, remove even the crumb of trust from them.

DETER THREATS FROM ATTACKING YOU

Where avoidance is control over your own presence and activities, deterrence is a degree of control over the presence and activities of others. Although you certainly can't directly control a person or make him leave you alone, you can indirectly affect his decision to target you.

One way this is done is by **"target hardening"**, which is making you more difficult to successfully attack without consequence. Most criminals would prefer to attack someone who will not fight back, or is too weak to defend him- or herself against the attack (this is why many thugs gang up on one lone victim – to increase their chance for success over their prey). Since what the bad guy wants is an easy target, we present to him a difficult one, so that he is more likely to look elsewhere. Here are some ways you can harden yourself against a violent attack:

Denial of Access: One

Of the most basic security principles states that the fewer people that have access to any given item, the more secure it becomes, assuming of course that the people who do have access to it are trustworthy. The same holds true in your private life. If you have not tested a person and are unsure of their loyalty to you, or if you have found that they are not trustable, they should not have access to you, your family, your home, or your valuables. The easiest method of separating yourself from outside threats is to go home, go inside, and lock the doors and windows; keep the bad guys outside and they can't easily take what's inside. If you're away from home, say at the grocery store, your safest location will usually be inside your vehicle with the doors locked and windows rolled up (don't forget to close the sunroof!), and a moving vehicle is a lot harder to steal from than a parked one. If these two options are not viable for your current situation, just remember, if you can put a locked door between you and the threat, you just made it harder for him to attack.

That is why I recommend that at the mall or grocery store people place their purchases in the trunks of their vehicles. It is why at home you should always lock your doors and windows, and in your car as well. And it is for this reason that we keep certain items of value locked safely away in a vault. However, you should know that doors, locks, and even security vaults are not intended to be the last line of defense, through which no criminal can ever pass. They are regarded in the security profession as simply delay devices; they slow down the attacker until a response team can arrive. Most high-end security vaults are only rated to delay a continuous, skillful attack for up to 12 hours. Which leads me to the next point:

Defensibility

As I have repeated many times now (what can I say? I love to drive home a point!), predatory people like attacking people who are less likely to be able to defend themselves. It is for this reason that many criminals work in groups and prefer to target lone females and elderly people. So it only stands to reason that a person who actually *is* able to effectively defend herself probably won't be targeted. Having to pick their own teeth up off the sidewalk is not on the to-do list of most criminals, so they generally stay away from people who they believe to be especially able to defend themselves. This includes police officers, military members, boxers, martial artists, body builders and gun enthusiasts, to name a few. Of course, this is generally speaking and does not apply in all situations. I've known soldiers who did not pay attention to their surroundings and got robbed at the ATM just outside of Fort Gordon, Georgia. And I've seen plenty of martial artists who weren't able to apply their skills on the street, either because the skills they learned were not effective, or because they did not have enough confidence in their skills to use them when the chips hit the fans.

If you are not inclined to change your profession and become a cop or join the military, you can still learn self-defense, or take up shooting if it is legal in your area. The confidence you gain from learning martial arts and/or shooting a handgun proficiently is priceless, and it's fun for most people, especially prior victims of violent assaults. Of course, it's not a good idea to go out and seek revenge on anyone - that makes you a criminal who is no better than the predators I'm teaching you to avoid, and you will get arrested for it.

Strength in Numbers

The great thing about the police force and the military (and unfortunately gangs and organized crime) is, there is strength in numbers. The same rule applies in your life as well. Criminals usually target those victims who are alone because of their vulnerability. Someone who is alone may not be able to reach out for help until it's too late. However, groups of people are harder to overcome than individuals, so it's always a good idea to travel with a buddy or two.

SELF PROTECTION

The U.S. Army calls this the "battle buddy system" - any time a soldier goes anywhere on or off base, he is to take another soldier of the same sex for increased safety. This is definitely a good idea for anyone, military or civilian, young, old, or middle aged. Children and teens should always be paired with a sibling or trusted friend of the same sex when engaging in activities not involving the parents outside the home. This will reduce kidnappings in addition to bullying and robberies. Adults who are of legal drinking age should make it a point to only drink with buddies, at least one of which agrees to be a designated driver. They should also refrain from traveling alone, even short distances. Your buddy can be a family member, coworker, spouse, or trusted friend. By utilizing the "battle buddy system", you can not only deter criminals from targeting you, but you will also have backup who can respond or call for help in case something does happen.

Another good way to deter crime is to address the issue of supply and demand. The vast majority of criminals attack for a material reason: they want something you have. Most want cash, but if cash isn't available they will settle for anything that can be quickly and easily converted into cash. This could be jewelry, electronics, credit and debit cards, tools, firearms, or personal information. The best way to avoid being targeted for these types of crimes is to conceal your valuables. Flashing a large sum of cash is a surefire way to get yourself noticed and possibly robbed, and when you wear expensive clothes and jewelry, you're essentially advertising to everyone, "hey! I have money! Come and get it!" Certainly, I would not suggest dressing in rags if you don't have to, but there is a time and a place for your Tiffany diamond bracelet and Wal-Mart on a Saturday evening may not be it. To prevent being targeted, be sure *to keep these valuables out of sight.* Carry only small amounts of cash with you (less than $100 is preferred), and don't allow others to see it. Only wear expensive-looking jewelry when necessary, and keep electronics such as cell phones, media players, and computers out of the public eye. When it comes to thieves, removing the opportunity to steal is one of the best methods of prevention. Out of sight, out of mind.

When all is said and done, a weak defense is better than nothing. Confidence is a huge deterrent to those criminals who seek an easy target. A person with confidence walks with a purpose, holds his or her head high, and makes eye contact with others. And remember, most predatory criminals don't want to target people who aren't afraid.

A lot of my childhood was spent dealing with social anxiety, being afraid to talk to people my age. I lacked confidence, and I was constantly targeted by bullies because of it. Once I began taking Karate classes, I actually searched for people to fight, and therefore inadvertently displayed my newfound confidence. No longer was I the target of bullies.

Suppose, however, that you haven't been taking Karate classes, and are not naturally confident. What then? My best advice for you is to fake it. It can be difficult at first, but with practice you can actually *become* confident just by regularly pretending that you are already confident. Walk, talk, and act like a confident person – chin up, not looking down or avoiding eye contact; walk with reason and direction, don't shuffle or drag your feet, and don't ever appear to be lost, confused, or unsure. You should make it obvious to everyone that you are alert, aware and vigilant, by continuously looking around; paying attention to everything that takes place within your line of sight. As they say, keep your head on a swivel. Make eye contact with as many people as are in your speaking range (10 or 15 feet). If someone is looking at you, make eye contact, smile and greet them with a businesslike "hello" or nod of your head, and keep walking. Make sure your hands are not in your pockets, but relaxed and swinging by your side.

I've heard that one effective method of walking with outward confidence is to imagine you are wearing a superhero's cape! Imagine the bravery of Superman or Superwoman as you walk through the mall, your cape flowing behind you! When standing, it can be a good idea to place your hands on your hips, which gives the impression that you are larger than you really are. You appear to take up more space and therefore are, in theory, more capable of defending yourself. Animals do this "posturing" in nature. A good example is when a cat feels threatened by a dog. The cat will raise its haunches, arch its back, and its fur stands up, all making the kitty look larger and more ferocious. A more timid dog may see this and decide that the cat isn't worth the trouble and retreat. It doesn't always turn out this way, but it's better than lying down and accepting defeat. The most important thing is to never show fear or uncertainty. Predators feed on that. Push those feelings back and show confidence instead.

DETECT/IDENTIFY THREATS

Detection, in a facility security sense, refers to being notified when a threat presents itself or a loss event occurs, such as an intruder breaking into a building. The burglar breaks open a window or door, which sets off an alarm and notifies the response team. Once the trespasser has gained entrance, a surveillance system should be able to record his actions and allow investigators to identify him so that if he gets away he can still be caught and brought to justice. In a personal security sense, detection and identification work the same way. However, we do not have electronic alarm and surveillance systems mounted on our bodies so we must use what we have to our advantage in order to keep us safe.

Although avoidance and deterrence are highly effective, they cannot stop a determined attacker. I may reasonably presume that a crowded mall on a Saturday afternoon is a well-lit, highly-populated public place and therefore is not a dangerous place, but earlier this year a mall in Columbia, Maryland was targeted by a young man who seemed determined to reenact the Columbine school shooting. An otherwise safe environment quickly turned deadly and chaotic. And in 2008, a Knoxville, Tennessee church – a place where most people consider to be inherently safe – was the scene of a horrible shooting that left two dead and seven wounded. I bring up these two tragic incidents only to drive home a point: nowhere is truly 100% sacred or safe from bad people intent on hurting others. Predators will find prey, and they will find a way to victimize them. Avoidance and deterrence alone will not stop them.

So, you have avoided most dangerous people, and you have taken steps to deter dangerous situations, and here you are standing in what you deem to be a safe place. What more can you possibly do now to further protect yourself? This is where awareness plays a leading role. In the Army we call it situational awareness, or SA. Awareness is the first line of defense and it's the most effective defensive measure anyone can ever take. Now here's what you should be aware of.

From across the crowded dance floor I saw the hand; a single horizontal wave of what appeared to be a fist. There were at least five hundred patrons crammed into a nightclub rated to safely contain only two hundred, and with the colored strobe lights there was no way to see exactly what was going on. I was one of eight security officers working that night – the very first night the Bears and Bulls Club in Birmingham, Alabama opened as a hip-hop club after failing as a honky-tonk. The night had been relatively eventless, but not uninteresting; the new owner was very tolerant concerning illegal drugs and prostitution and the security team was instructed to "look the other way." While reluctantly looking the other way I saw something out of the ordinary; an unnatural movement among the patrons. The crowd seemed to coalesce around something, which was a sure sign that a fight was imminent. With a heightened awareness I searched the crowd for the source. And then I saw the fist. I began to move toward the fight, and as I pushed through the horde of drunken dancers, the club seemed to distort around me. The DJ was playing the Three 6 Mafia song, "*Tear Da Club Up*", and they were certainly taking the lyrics literally. It was like something you see in an old Western movie; beer bottles flying through the air, people slinging chairs and knocking over tables. Three of the five security guards that were watching the dance floor sprayed pepper spray indiscriminately into the crowd, which emptied the club in seconds. At 2:24 a.m. the Bears and Bulls Club shut its doors for the night – twenty-four minutes late and six minutes after the last patron left complaining about being pregnant and allergic to pepper spray.

While it is easy to read a group of people on a crowded dance floor, it can be more difficult to read individual people or ones in smaller groups. However, the principles are basically the same. Watch for unnatural movements. Do you see signs of anger – rapid body motions, pointing or swinging hand motions, wild flailing of the arms, or sprinting towards another person? Do you hear shouting or cursing that sounds angry? And pay attention to the actions of the crowd, people generally are drawn to the scene of a fight or struggle. Take note if people seem particularly attracted to a single area. These signs can indicate that someone is physically attacking another person. The attack may not concern you, but you should be aware of it so that you don't inadvertently wander into harm's way. Gunshots could possibly follow such an exchange and you definitely don't want to be anywhere near if that happens.

You should be aware of the presence and location of anyone and everyone you can see. You should also know when someone faces you, stares at you, or moves toward you. This could mean that the person is targeting you for an attack, however, they may be completely innocent. An accurate prediction can usually be determined by what the person is carrying (if anything) and how he approaches. If the person is dressed well and carrying a nonweapon product, pamphlet, computer, or brief case in hand, and is approaching you directly from the front, he's probably a professional salesman or business owner just trying to make a living. Conversely, if someone sneaks up on you from behind you yet with nothing in his hands, there may be cause for concern. And if anyone is approaching you from any angle with a weapon drawn you should definitely take notice.

Maintaining a safe distance is very important in detecting attacks ahead of time. When approached by someone you don't know (or don't trust), you should always keep a "*reactionary gap*" which means that you shouldn't let anyone get within four to six feet of you; if he can touch you, he's too close. If you don't set physical boundaries and enforce them, people will invade your space and assault you, pick your pockets, or make you feel just plain uncomfortable. Keep them at bay and make sure they don't get a chance to get too close. It could save your life.

RESPOND TO ATTACKS

Response deals primarily with taking action once an attack has been initiated. In a corporate environment, when a security alarm indicates that a person has gained access to an area without permission, a security team will respond very quickly. The response team must act promptly. It's a race against time to keep the damage to a minimum.

Much like the corporate example, you must be able to respond to personal attacks quickly and take the appropriate action to minimize your damages. Your response will depend on the individual circumstances of the attack, and will be determined to a large degree by the law and your personal abilities. While each situation is different, there are some fairly universal methods to responding to an attack.

The first and absolute best thing you can do in response to an attack is to place distance between you and the threat. While the perpetrator has physical access to you, he will have opportunity to do physical and emotional harm. But if you separate yourself from the bad guy the attack will have to cease. This can be done by walking or running away, or in some cases making the adversary leave. Reiterating what was said in the section on deterrence, the easiest method of separating yourself from a physical threat is to place a locked door between you and the threat. Although we are no longer dealing with a threat, but an active physical attack, this principle holds doubly true.

The separation principle also applies to proprietary attacks; if you remove access to your valuables, the attack must cease. If someone is attempting to steal something which belongs to you, or vandalize your property, simply deny them access to those items. Place a fence around your property to keep vandals away, or lock your valuables away in a safe place. The mechanism you use to secure your property need not be expensive; it just has to be strong enough to hold back the intruder.

In the case of an environmental attack – let's take cyber bullying for example, denial of access works just as well. If you remove the troublemaker from your list of people who have access to your social media, block them from calling or texting your phone, or shut down your current social media account, there isn't much the person can do to continue their assault on you. According to the cyber bullying response website *www.deletecyberbullying.org*, you should ignore minor teasing and name calling (which, by the way is its own form of access denial), and according to the National Crime Prevention Council, victims of cyber bullying should stop all communications with the bully or bullies whenever possible.

While removing access works very well against physical, proprietary, and environmental attacks, it works only marginally well against reputational attacks. However, it does have a positive effect. Most reputational attacks are caused by outsiders, some even ex-insiders who have had a falling out with the target. The attacker spreads rumors about the victim, most of which may be based on some misconstruction of reality or possibly completely true, but with a twist. While many people do tell flat-out made up lies, what the victim needs to realize is that any and all information provided to the offender can and will be used against them in some form or fashion. Therefore, by removing access to you and your information, you are effectively removing ammunition from the loudmouth who is causing trouble for you. Coincidentally, placing distance between you and the situation also removes the emotional effects that knowing about the attacks has on you, and that's even better for you in the long run.

Your next response to attacks should be to alert your response force. Your response force will vary with your individual lifestyle and circumstances. When speaking with Hartley Peavey about his facility security, I asked him if there was anything he wanted me to do to improve his personal security. His reply to me was, "I *am* my own security," which, to a large degree is true for Hartley. However, should Mr. Peavey ever need protecting, he does have at his disposal a well-trained, very capable security team, ready to go to war for him should he ever make the call.

While many executives do have bodyguards at their sides, most of us can't afford such elaborate personal protection. And while some of us are very capable of protecting ourselves and our families, there are so many who are not physically able to do so. Whether you believe you are fully capable or somewhat challenged in physical ability, you should have a response force; you should have backup in case of an attack. Luckily for you, there is just such a response team on duty twenty-four hours a day, seven days a week, just waiting for your call. That team is your local police. If you are being attacked physically or proprietarily, you can call the police and press charges.

However, if your reputation is being wrongly attacked, the police will have little to say about it. In that case it is best to call an attorney. Likewise, the local police may not have the training or authority to handle certain cybercrimes – criminal offenses like computer intrusion (hacking), child pornography or exploitation, internet fraud or SPAM, internet harassment, and internet bomb threats. These would best be handled by your Federal Bureau of Investigation (FBI) local office.

While I do not believe that violence is the answer, sometimes you have to fight back in order to survive. This pertains only to physical attacks, of course. You must be knowledgeable of Federal, State, and municipal laws before you act so as to decrease your chances of being a victim of both the criminal and the criminal justice system. For the sake of this book, I will say that violence should be your very last option, and you should only fight back physically if your life or someone else's life is in danger. Otherwise I would advise against fighting back with physical force. Actual self-defense principles and techniques will be covered later in the book, under Lessons 4 and 5, *Self-Defense Principles* and *Weapons*.

ASSESS INCIDENTS TO LEARN FROM THE EXPERIENCE

Assessment occurs after a known attack has been attempted, whether the attack was successful or not. The goal is to find out as much about the incident in order to recover some or all of the assets and resources lost, prevent further losses, and to learn more effective responses to certain situations. In the military we called this an after action review, or AAR. Without this assessment, the wealth of information provided by your attacker will go to waste and you will most certainly become a repeat victim. Villains will see you as a particularly easy target and they will come out of the woodwork to attack you. Here are some useful questions to ask after an attack:

Who?

Who was involved? Who was attacked? Who performed the attack? Knowing who was involved can help you pinpoint motives and methods and implement new strategies to help protect the victim(s) of this attack in the future. Knowing who your attacker was will also tell you who to avoid in the future, so that you are no longer a victim of that person.

What?

What kind of attack was it? What happened, exactly? What was lost or damaged? Finding out this information is important because each individual circumstance carries with it a unique set of variables which dictates how you will respond to it. You must find out what assets were targeted so that you can protect those assets in the future. Also, knowing exactly what has been lost or damaged is the first step in recovering those items.

When?

When did the attack take place? Was it a crime of opportunity, enacted by a split-second decision, or was it a carefully planned and orchestrated over a period of days, weeks, or months? Once you know this, you can begin to strengthen your defenses.

Where?

Where did the attack occur? This knowledge can help you determine what places you deem safe and what locations are dangerous. Although you can't expect to avoid every place in which there is an attack, you can be especially alert during your time spent in those places.

Why?

Why was this crime committed? We often are not privy to the motives of our attackers. But we may be able to find out why the victim was targeted. Was he or she especially vulnerable? Was he or she simply in the wrong place at the wrong time, or was he or she involved in activities or associations that encouraged the attack? Perhaps the victim had not read this book and did not know how to prevent the attack!

How?

Understanding the methods of your attacker can give you invaluable insight into defeating further attempts. If you know that a burglar entered your house through an open window, from then on, your windows should always be closed and locked. Study what has happened and try to ascertain just how the attacker was able to enact the crime.

Sustains

In an effective after action review, you should ask the questions listed above, and then analyze the answers. Try to find three (or at least two) things that went well, whether it's how calm you stayed in the face of danger, or making the decision to call 911 at just the right time. These are called "sustains"; they are the things that you will want to repeat if a similar incident repeats itself.

Improves

Now we get to the meat of the review, which is knowing what to improve in the future. Take a look at all the questions you just asked yourself about the incident that you are assessing. Who? What? When? Where? Why? And how? Take a look at the things that went well, the things you did right. Now examine what could have been done differently to make a difference. Make sure that all the improvements you come up. Be realistic. Are the improvements you have come up with feasible? Can you afford them? Do you have the support of your family or friends? Can you improve anything right now, before the next incident? Be honest with yourself, and leave pride out of the equation. Everyone can improve somehow. Now is the time to find out how you can improve.

GOING FORWARD; APPLYING LESSONS LEARNED

Now that you have assessed the situation, it's time to recover your losses, if any, and after lessons learned put the whole thing behind you.

Recovery

If you have sustained any losses, now is the time to attempt to recover them. If your bank account has been drained, contact the bank. The FDIC should have insured your money. If your house or vehicle has been damaged, contact your insurance agency. And for your own safety, please seek medical attention if you have been injured even slightly. Recovery in any form can take a long time, and the longer you wait to begin, the more difficult it is to fully recover. Some damages to the house that go unfixed can get worse with time, vehicles rust, and our human bodies compensate for damages and break down until the situation gets far worse than it has to be.

I received a significant blow to my jaw in my late teens during a fight, and I was certain that my jaw had gotten dislocated. From that moment forward my jaw audibly popped every time I ate. It didn't hurt, so I thought little of it; in fact, I was proud of my battle injury! But as time went on, my jaw muscles opposite the injury began to compensate for the abnormal positioning. Just this year I began having severe pain in my neck, shoulder, and head. A visit to an oral surgeon, x-rays of the affected area, and a special TMJ splint device cost me a lot of money that I could have saved, had I gotten the problem fixed much sooner. The lesson: don't neglect your health. It only gets worse with time.

Continuity of Life

A big part of going forward after a violent or traumatic attack is seeing to your emotional well-being. A life-threatening attack can be unnerving at best, but at worst can result in Post-Traumatic Stress Disorder (PTSD), which causes a person to feel unsafe or helpless. Most people associate PTSD with soldiers who have seen combat, but civilians and even children can experience the condition once known as "shell shock". Post-Traumatic Stress Disorder can affect any person who experiences an upsetting event, someone who witnesses it, emergency response personnel, and even the friends and family of the victim. It can be caused by a combat experience, natural disaster, a serious vehicle accident, rape or assault, the sudden death of a loved one, or childhood neglect, among other things.

According to the National Institute of Mental Health (NIMH), Post-Traumatic Stress Disorder can bring with it the following symptoms:

1. Re-experiencing the traumatic event through flashbacks, bad dreams, or frightening thoughts.
2. Avoiding reminders of the trauma. Victims may feel emotionally numb, or may feel strong guilt, depression, or worry. They may lose interest in activities they once deeply enjoyed, and they may have a hard time remembering the dangerous event.
3. Increased anxiety and emotional arousal, as evidenced by being easily startled, feeling tense or "on edge", having intense outbursts of anger, and/or difficulty sleeping.

If you or someone you know is experiencing what you suspect to be PTSD, please seek help as soon as possible. The sooner PTSD is confronted, the easier it is to overcome. Please know that seeking help dealing with the aftermath of a life-threatening event is not a sign of weakness, and the only way to overcome it is to confront it and, with the help of an experienced therapist or doctor, to learn to accept the event as a part of your past.

THE ADD/RAG PROCESS

Forgiveness

Can be the most difficult part of the Going Forward process. When someone has done you wrong, it is natural to feel animosity for that person and anyone who helped him or didn't help you. And it certainly is natural and even advisable that you don't trust someone who has committed a grave injustice against you. However, what we all must realize is that when you hold a grudge, you diminish your own emotional health, while the person who has done you wrong most likely receives none of what you are feeling. Maybe he feels bad about what he has done; perhaps he doesn't even realize he's done anything wrong. Quite possibly he feels absolutely no remorse for his actions. But regardless you have to go on living.

Studies show that one key to longevity and good health is to develop a mindset of gratitude and let go of past hurts. It's not that your attacker deserves forgiveness – but *you* do. You deserve to live free from the bondage of reliving this tragedy day in and day out. You deserve to be happy again, and it is impossible to do so while still holding onto the pain and hate you feel for your enemy. It is interesting to know that the Aramaic word for "forgive" means literally to "untie". Your unforgiveness emotionally ties you to the wrongdoer. By forgiving him, you can untie those binds and walk away, free to live your life without the bitterness that would otherwise consume you and darken your life.

Of course, forgiveness is not the same as forgetting the past; there is much to be learned from your tragedy, the most important perhaps being that the person who attacked you is not to be trusted. But you can retain the lessons without the pain, and you can apply those lessons to your future. But that does not mean that you have to let the person who hurt you back into your life. Far from it! Forgiveness simply means that you have let go of the ball and chain you once carried, it does not mean that a relationship needs to exist between the two participants.

The first step to forgiveness is realizing that the hate you feel isn't affecting the other person like it is affecting you. Remember, "Resentment is like drinking poison and waiting for it to kill your enemy." [Nelson Mandela]. Now, try to find something positive that has come from your experience. Perhaps you have become stronger, you've learned a lesson, or you made a new ally through this episode. Find the silver lining in the dark cloud, so to speak. Focus on the positives even when you really feel like focusing on the incident or your hate for the person that attacked you.

Speak the words, "I forgive you." You don't have to say it to the person, but say it aloud anyway. Say it every day if that's what it takes. Breathe deeply and let those feelings go. Grieve at your own pace, and don't bottle up your emotions. And then, over time you will begin to actually feel that you have forgiven this person for the evil he has paid you. It will be at that time that you can truly live again and put the whole episode behind you.

LESSON 3

EMERGENCY PLANNING AND PRACTICE

If you are to survive a catastrophic event, it helps to know how to respond to it. It takes planning and practice to program the proper reactions into your mind. Planning ahead involves learning from mistakes made by others and applying those lessons to your life. It also involves learning from your own experiences and applying those lessons to your plan. Your plan will be specific to your life and circumstances. Take into consideration all the people who depend on you to protect them – your children, your parents, your friends who may get caught up in the events surrounding you, their children, and their friends. Know that your actions and inactions don't just affect you, but many others around you. You should construct a plan that takes others' safety into consideration. Include them in discussions about your survival plan. Ask for their help; your friends and family can be a valuable resource in getting away from dangerous situations.

Make a safety plan for your children. Talk to them about your expectations and why it is important to follow the plan. Make up a code word for certain situations (my family's code word was "coaster" – the only time I remember it being used was when a person I did not know was asked to pick me up from school during a time of emergency. The person said the code word to let me know he was sent by my mom and it was ok to go with him). Code words can also be used to mean there is danger, signaling for the child to run and hide or seek help. The code words should be easy enough for the child to remember and you should discuss them periodically to ensure your child remembers them. If you can avoid doing so, do not change the code words, as this can cause confusion between you and your child.

Make a plan with your spouse also. A dear friend of mine, a police officer from Lafayette, Louisiana told me of an incident in which he and his family were out in public when a man approached them. The young man perhaps threateningly announced his recognition of my friend as a police officer. Troy motioned for his wife to take their two daughters and get in the vehicle, as he remained to sort out the man's intentions. Not a word needed to be spoken because Troy and his family already knew the drill. It is this kind of planning I speak of here.

Plan it out. What should you and your family do when there is danger? Take the strategy seriously and convey that urgency to your children. They may not understand it, but do not let them make light of the plan and your reasons for discussing it. Failure to plan could cost you your life or the life of a family member.

It never hurts to make a game out of your emergency strategy for the small children. Run an imaginary "danger drill" to get some practice and see how everything will work out. Don't be surprised when something doesn't go quite the way you planned; it rarely goes perfectly, and that isn't always a bad thing. When things go wrong during practice, it allows you to discuss and make adjustments to the strategy.

Your plan should include a few different scenarios. What would you and your family do if someone broke into your house while you were home? Where can you all go to hide or escape? What would you do during a natural disaster? What would you do if, while out with your family someone dangerous approached you? Getting your children to safety should be your first priority, followed by your spouse or other family members, and lastly, yourself. However, the optimal condition would be all members of the family getting to safety as a unit – that is, at the same time. Try to consider all the options, and choose the one that best suits your most likely situations.

LESSON 4

SELF-DEFENSE BASICS

Although avoidance is always better than response, there are times when a physical attack is unavoidable. It is for that reason I have decided to include a section on self-defense. This section will read much like the classes I have taught for nearly a decade. However, without having to conform to the time constraints of a short class period, I will also be expanding on many of the elements that I mention nearly in passing in some of my classes. Please note that, although much more informative, this book (or any portion of it) is no replacement for professional instruction and supervised practice. The methods and techniques described herein are dangerous and can result in serious injury and death. This section is intended only for reference and not to replace professional instruction.

That being said, the goal of any combat scenario is to survive. Certainly, law enforcement officers, soldiers, correctional officers and security guards alike all want to control their surroundings and dominate on the battle field. But at the end of the day most of them will consider themselves lucky to just make it back home. Since this book is written with the non-protective professional in mind, we will set our sights on simply surviving. Many people are not willing or able to carry firearms with them to public places, due to state laws or their own moral standards. They do not have a Taser on their side, or pepper spray in a pouch on their utility belt. In addition, it would be impractical to expect a book to transform anyone into a professional fighter capable of going toe-to-toe and winning a street fight against someone who outweighs them. So, it is my duty to arm you, not with a firearm or non-lethal weapon, but with knowledge. You already have the weapons – your hands, feet, knees, elbows, and head – you just have to know how to use them effectively. It is my sincere hope that I can aid you in learning how to do just that so you can survive a physical attack long enough to escape and find safety.

There are many, many martial arts styles and self-defense systems available to the public. I have studied a few and know from my own firsthand experience that the majority of them are commercialized, watered-down, crap. I began learning Shotokan Karate in 1997 under the instruction of a classmate whose parents owned and operated the small independent dojo, a nonprofit organization funded by grants and donations. Most of their students were not the upper- and middle-class children who were simply bored and wanted to become Power Rangers; they were the lower-class kids whose families could not afford to attend the world certified Han Mu Do class, or the high-class Tae Kwon Do academy that a lot of the rich kids spent less than a year in. I started taking Karate classes specifically because I wanted to learn to defend myself against the many bullies who plagued me at school.

After two years of thrice weekly attendance (if the doors were open, I was inside the dojo), I had earned my purple belt, which was just two belts from black, and I was a star student. I was told by everybody there that if I could go to all the tournaments in one season, I would most certainly bring home a championship. I was working hard to earn my black belt, helping to teach other students what the instructors had a hard time imparting, and learning what I assumed to be self-defense in the process.

SELF-DEFENSE BASICS

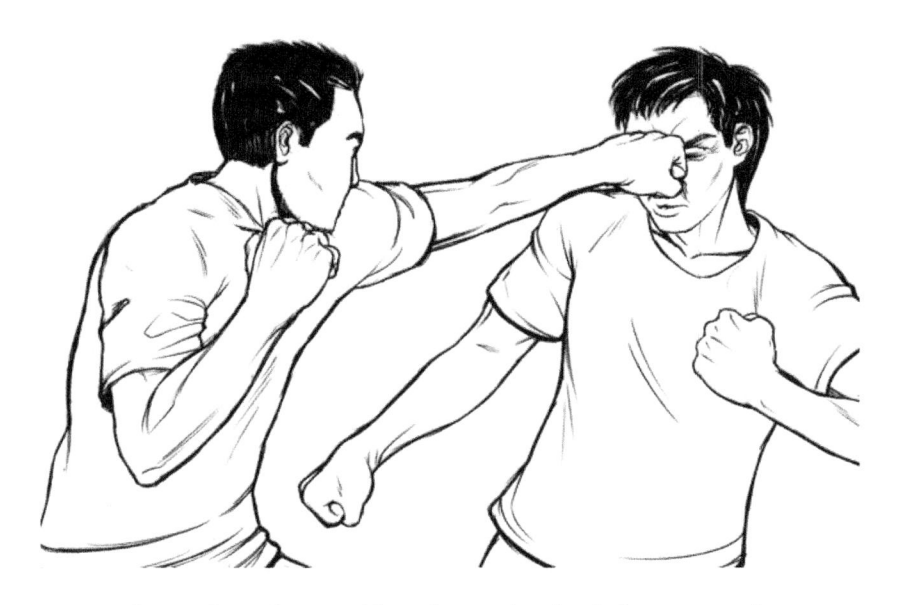

One day I found myself making the bad decision of getting into a fight that wasn't even mine. I had just returned home from Karate class and the police were at our neighbor's house arresting two men, for what I don't know. One of the men was in handcuffs and the police attempted to arrest the other one, but he ran. That man led the two police officers on a foot chase in circles around the house, throwing trash cans and other debris in his path. I decided that since Shotokan Karate was designed to be an aid to justice, I should lend my talents to the cause of law and order. I ran ahead of the fleeing suspect and turned to him, my hand out toward him signaling him to stop. Two years in Karate had surely prepared me to fight if the need arose, but he didn't seem like much of a threat. I'd taken down my 250-pound instructors with expert moves that inflicted massive pain and left them rubbing their joints. I was ready, and this was my moment. I saw nothing. I just felt what seemed like a jolt of electricity burst through my body, and I was unable to stand. I dropped, face first into the street as the perpetrator ran past without even breaking stride. I pulled myself painfully to my feet and went to report to the police officer who was radioing the incident to dispatch. I warned him that I believed the man to have used a stun gun on me, but he quickly corrected me: the man had not shocked me with a stun gun, but had simply punched me in the mandibular angle, a pressure point located behind the jaw hinge, just below the ear. That was my very first real life encounter with pressure points. I had been told by my Karate instructors that they were not effective. I had just learned a firsthand lesson to the contrary. I was sorely disillusioned by my training and inability to defend myself.

When I returned to Karate class the next week, I told my instructors about the incident, and I asked them why I had failed to defend myself. I got the same prepackaged answer from each of my four instructors: "you have only begun to learn Karate; you've learned just enough to get into trouble." That was a disheartening answer after studying for two years and being the best student in my school. Finally, I asked the right person. Mike Mason, then a first degree Black Belt, told me that not all Karate is taught with the goal of self-defense in mind. What I had been learning was tournament Karate, and it was not practical for self-defense purposes. He agreed to take me under his wing and teach me the more "realistic" methods of Karate.

I wrote all this to illustrate how important it is to know what you are learning and to know the difference between commercialized tournament-oriented martial arts and combat effective self-defense systems. If I were pressed to recommend a self-defense program, I wouldn't have to think long before reaching a conclusion. For the money, Krav Maga is simply the best. It is an Israeli combat system, designed and proven on the battlefields of the Middle East. Its general lack of complicated, "flashy" moves that seem to populate every Asian martial art makes it inherently more combat effective than its Eastern cousins. That's not to say there are no other good programs available, but I believe this one to be the best system for the amount of money you will spend.

FIGHT PHYSIOLOGY

The human body and mind are complex systems designed to operate in various climates and conditions automatically. An example is found in weight lifting. Your body perceives the lifting of weights that are heavier than it is used to and it releases hormones to facilitate the effective lifting of those weights. As you lift those weights repeatedly it creates tiny micro-tears in the muscles. In response, your body sends proteins to the site of those tears in order to repair them and rebuild the muscles bigger than before so that in the future your muscles can lift those weights with greater ease.

Likewise, when you find yourself in danger, your mind perceives the danger and your body responds by releasing hormones to facilitate your survival. Many things happen almost simultaneously within your body. Upon perceiving a potentially life threatening situation, your sympathetic nervous system (SNS) is activated and adrenaline is released into the blood stream. At the same time, digestion and reproduction are temporarily halted in order to ensure the important systems are running at maximum efficiency for survival purposes in this moment. Blood is pooled into the head and torso so that the brain, heart, and lungs can remain active for a while, even if an extremity is cut or severed. You don't feel all that, but it happens.

What you do feel is the adrenaline dump. You feel the uneasiness in your stomach. You feel nervous tingling in your hands. You find it difficult to perform complex actions such as choosing the right key from a group and placing it into a small keyhole. As your heart rate increases to 145 beats per minute and higher, those complex actions become even more difficult, while gross motor skills – the ability to punch, kick, and run – become much easier. You experience what is known as "tunnel vision"; instead of seeing wide angles and being able to detect motion with your peripheral vision, you now are focused solely on the threat. Your depth perception is also distorted, making it difficult to see up close to properly aim a firearm. And among all the others, your hearing is distorted, a condition known as "auditory exclusion".

These things happen in the course of just seconds. And once you perceive life threatening danger and the SNS is activated, you have roughly 10-15 seconds of "burn time" in which your body will provide the necessary energy needed to either fight or run away. After that, there is a 45% decrease in output potential, and it continues to decrease until about 90 seconds into the event, you will only be able to perform at about 31% maximum efficiency for the remainder of the event. You will want to take advantage of the 10-15 seconds of maximum energy, because after that, exhaustion seems to come very quickly. Of course, that 10-15 seconds is only available to you if your mind and body are clear before the onset of the incident. If you are exhausted from work, sick, or under the influence of drugs or alcohol, you won't have the luxury of using that time to your benefit. You may never even realize you are in danger until it is too late, and when you do realize it, your body can't respond as effectively. You may only get three or four short seconds to enjoy your seemingly super-human strength. Or you may get none.

The activation of the sympathetic nervous system brings about the changes listed above, which is classified as "survival stress". There isn't much we can do about survival stress; it's hardwired into our bodies. It's there for a reason and it works pretty darn well. Unfortunately, the side effects seem to appear at the most inconvenient times. Although we can't turn off the SNS and prevent survival stress from occurring, we can take steps to reduce the negative effects of survival stress.

Tactical Breathing

"Humans suck at breathing." That is a statement I recently heard from a wellness coach during one of my collaborative self-defense classes, and it just happens to be true. As much practice as we get at it, we really don't breathe all that well when we leave our lungs on autopilot. It especially rings true in the midst of a very stressful situation in which your life is on the line. But breathing correctly is extremely important to our survival. Without giving you another lesson in anatomy and physiology, I'd like to point out the many times you notice yourself not breathing for several seconds, or breathing much harder than you should while holding a normal conversation or walking a moderate distance. Anyone who has suffered through an anxiety attack or panic attack can easily relate to just how difficult it can be to control your own breathing when everything should be working just fine.

But in the heat of battle, the correct breathing can relieve a lot of the negative side effects experienced under survival stress. I was originally taught to breathe tactically in response to anxiety attacks, but soon found out that it can be applied in other situations as well.

Count to three as you breathe in slowly through your nose. In, Mississippi...2, Mississippi...3, Mississippi.

Count to six as you breathe out slowly through your mouth. Out, Mississippi...2, Mississippi...3, Mississippi...4, Mississippi...5, Mississippi...6, Mississippi. Notice how relaxing it is. During times of great duress, breathing in a pattern similar to this will work to alleviate some of the chaos you experience within yourself as you struggle to make the right decisions.

Why? Because much of the symptoms of survival stress come about as a result of your heart rate. When your heart reaches 115 beats per minute (BPM) as a result of a perceived threat, the sympathetic nervous system is activated, which releases adrenaline and other hormones, and fine motor skills (those movements that involve dexterity and hand-eye coordination) begin to deteriorate. As your heart rate increases, dexterity further disappears and it becomes difficult for you to do anything but the most basic things such as running and punching. However, when you slow your breathing, you slow your heart rate, and it reduces some of the effects of survival stress.

Confidence in Your Abilities

Tactical breathing alone won't eliminate all the symptoms of survival stress, no matter how "tactically" you breathe. However, those with a high level of confidence in themselves and their ability to defend themselves and survive are far less likely to perceive certain dangers as life-threatening. This in turn results in a delayed or reduced activation of the SNS.

Take for instance, my run-in with a knife-wielding woman intent on cutting another woman in an apartment complex in DeKalb, Mississippi back in 2010. As soon as I realized that a knife was involved, my training kicked in and I drew my handgun. My stance changed from upright and natural, to that of a boxer as I went into "fight" mode. I was prepared long before that moment to take a life if that is what was necessary. I was too close to too many people to present my weapon at arm's length, and somehow I cognitively knew it. Instead, I kept the gun close to my center, pointing it down away from everyone until I was absolutely certain I would have to use it. My breathing was slow. I was relaxed. I knew what to do and I didn't have to think about it. But I still had tunnel vision. I heard nothing more than the muffled collective crowd around me. That is, until I heard the faint, distinctive "clink" of the knife hitting the ground.

You see, in this incident I had a great deal of confidence in my abilities. I had trained for this moment for over a decade. I used to hope for an incident like this one, back when I was new to the security guard profession. The confidence I had which was made possible by my excellent training gave me a calmness, a state of knowing. Without that training I could have frozen up or perhaps shot imprudently into the crowd. Realistic training and practice is very important to gaining confidence in chips-hit-the-fans scenarios.

Another, perhaps more effective way to gain confidence is through real-world experience. Although much more dangerous, a single successful experience can instantly boost certainty within one's self and continued success has a monumentally adverse effect on fear. However, I would not advise anyone to seek out opportunities to face real violence simply for the experience. The safest and most logical way to gain confidence would be to seek out good quality training opportunities and learn all you can about self-protection from the safety of a controlled environment.

While I was in the Army, part of my hand-to-hand combat training involved "the clinch drill" – an exercise in which drill sergeants donned boxing gloves and beat the living daylights out of the students, one on one style. Our job as pupils was to "close the gap" and clinch the drill sergeant so that he could not effectively strike. We were not allowed to strike the sergeants, only to clinch them until we were given the command by a referee to release. I had never fought a boxer before and had therefore never been struck by a boxing glove, only lightly punched by martial artists with relatively light and controlled force. Even though I knew we were in a controlled setting, and I knew the referees would not allow us to get seriously injured, I was watching students get knocked unconscious, I saw teeth get knocked out, and lots of noses got broken that day. I felt plenty of fear as I stepped up to clinch my first of four opponents. I combined the training I had received at Fort Benning with that of my many years in martial arts and defensive tactics. I received a few good taps in the face and quickly fought through the fear to affect the clinch. Once I realized that getting punched in the face doesn't hurt as much as people make it out to, I threw fear to the wind and breezed through the second and third clinches. And then there was the fourth and final clinch cycle. I had watched this drill sergeant take out soldiers left and right. He had an intimidating way about him; he was enjoying this way too much. He stood upright and arrogant, dropping his left hand to the front, dangling it teasingly. As the students stepped up and secured their mouth guards, he smiled and told them, "I'm going to hit you with this hand, right here, and there's nothing you can do about it." He would sometimes place his right hand behind his back as if to take it out of the fight. I watched students step up and get cold-cocked by the very hand the sergeant had just warned them about! It was a fearful sight, but having had the opportunity to watch his methods, I was slightly more prepared for the trick. Finally it was my turn. I stepped up, still afraid of the pain that I just might have to endure at the hands of this merciless warrior. Fully expecting that first punch – the one that had so far not missed a single face – I took a step into punching range. I watched his shoulder roll forward hard and fast; I instinctively blocked and moved my upper body off the line of attack and watched as the battering ram of a fist flew by my head and stopped just above me. I saw the surprise on his face, and then I rushed in to grab him. I felt the pride swell within me. I had just done what none of my classmates had: I had dodged the "thunder punch!" And then I felt the right hand slam into my face like a sledge hammer. I let go of the drill sergeant's shirt and stumbled back. Clearly, his right hook was much worse than his left uppercut. My head was spinning and my ears ringing. I felt the warm blood flow from my nose and down my face. I wiped the blood off my face with my bare arm and found my opponent circling, jumping and dancing with joy. As unpleasant as it was, I realized that I didn't feel any actual pain, just a good old fashioned "rung bell". I figured getting hit again could do some real damage, so I had to end this quickly. I rushed in and achieved the clinch before he could knock me out.

This experience changed me. Not only am I braver and more confident, I now know I can take a hit and keep going. In fact, before the training I had cat-like reflexes and was prone to block my friends' random punches, slaps, and attempts to grab me in various playful headlocks and choke holds without notice. Now I don't even bother. Instead I simply launch a counterattack and take the hit to the face. I've lost a large portion of my fear and it shows. It's just one of the side effects of good quality training.

Visualization Drills

It began as a fantasy; I imagined getting accosted by the bullies. I thought of ways I could defeat them, humiliate them, and most of all make them think twice about messing with me again. I envisioned the techniques I had been trained to perform. It played out a lot like the opening scene in "Sherlock Holmes" (2009): the bully accosts me from a distance; I talk smack and lure him into punching me first (which is a really bad idea in real life!). He punches, I block. Counter with a punch to the stomach. He doubles over in pain, and I use his forward motion to throw him to the ground. Stepping on his throat just enough to cause severe discomfort, I tell him to leave me alone or next time I will break bones. Ok, so it's not the most realistic fight scene I ever imagined (let's keep this PG, shall we?), but it was a start. I didn't know it at the time, but daydreaming about what I would do if someone attacked me was a form of training.

In the 1960's, Professor L.V. Clark of Wayne State University studied two groups of basketball players over a two-week period: those who practiced by shooting free-throws each morning, and those who engaged in "mental practice", visualizing making shots but not actually doing real practice. Both groups improved their free-throw shooting. Further research has shown that imagery can produce better performance outcomes and have a positive effect on anxiety, motivation, and self-efficacy. While visualization is not replacement for actual practice and training, it is a good supplement to your training.

Start with a scenario: a setting. Maybe you are at the grocery store. Think about the store, its layout, and pedestrian and vehicular traffic. Where did you park? Now let's progress. You have all the items you came for, you've paid for them, and now you're walking to your car. You've followed all the other advice in this book and your head is on a swivel. You see everything. You see the grocery store employee taking a smoke break in front of the store. You see a lot of people who seem nearly oblivious to their surroundings as they walk from their vehicles to the store and vice versa. You see a man sitting in his vehicle about five cars down from yours, presumably waiting for his wife while she shops. As you near your vehicle, someone approaches you from behind and asks you for ten dollars to get some gas. Since you don't carry cash on you, you tell him nicely that you don't have it. He persists abrasively. "I know you got money. Gimme ten to get some gas with."

What would you do? Visualize the whole scene. Make sure your chosen responses are realistic, and imagine going through the actions. For example, it would not likely be realistic to imagine you turning cartwheels across a parking lot in order to end up flip-kicking your assailant in his face, then standing over him as you issue a superhero sized warning to him about correcting his behavior (now that you have that image in your head, remove it and let's start thinking outside the Hollywood box!).

Now let's take that imagination a bit further. Imagine you are at home. It's just you and the kids (if you don't have kids, pretend you do). Someone kicks open your door and rushes in; it's a home invasion! The man is much bigger than you and he obviously means to do some harm. What will you do? The man is aggressive and fast; there is no time to go to another room to grab a weapon. Do you have one on you? Think it through and come up with a plan.

The objective here isn't really planning your fight; whatever you plan, you can with great certainty bet that something will go wrong. The goal here is to train your mind to make a decision now for an event that may occur later. It helps to build your confidence, and it "programs" your brain to create a solution to a possible problem, so that if/when the problem presents itself, your brain can begin to solve it much faster. It works for basketball teams, martial artists, military units, and people like you and me. Just remember to keep it realistic as you can, and don't go overboard with the slaughter and mayhem. Playing out your fantasy of ripping out intestines and feeding them to your attacker will most assuredly get you in a lot of trouble with the law!

Positive Mindset

One of the most effective reducers of survival stress is having a positive mindset, believing in yourself or a cause, and having hope for a positive outcome. This doesn't begin the moment you find yourself in distress; it begins right now. Positive thinking is a continual lifestyle decision that occurs each day. Right now, as you read this book, decide for yourself what you are capable of, what you are willing to do, and what your purpose for survival is. Who are you surviving for? What will keep you alive when your physical abilities are exhausted, and you're lying on the ground, your life blood beneath you?

Hope is a powerful thing – hope in humanity, hope in a brighter future, faith in God, knowing that win or lose, live or die, the world will continue to turn and things will get better. In times of great tragedy, whether we are staring death in the face at the end of a gun barrel, or we are barely clinging to life beneath the debris of a devastating natural disaster, it is not just our weapons or our knowledge that we will cling to; it is our hope. Hope is what motivates brave soldiers to do things that turn the tides of war. Hope is what motivates people to survive in the wilderness when the rest of their party is dead. And hope is what brings us through prolonged hardship, be it enduring financial ruin or a shattered family. I encourage you to find something to have faith in today if you have not already done so.

I have several sources of hope; my first and most influential source of hope is God. It is my faith in Him that allows me to live my life without fear, knowing that even if I die today I have lived my life to the fullest every chance I've gotten, and I've served God and others to the best of my ability, abiding by Jesus's commandments to "Love God with all your heart, soul, and mind," and "Love your neighbor as yourself."

Another source of hope for me is my little sister. She has been my anchor and my reason for trying to be a good person when my inner selfishness tries to rise up. She will probably be the face I see if I ever truly face mortality up close and personal. Even now I can imagine the distress on her face, tears streaming over my death. That thought alone makes me want to run faster, fight harder, do one more pushup, two more sit ups, and train like my life depends on it – because it does.

Find your source. Find it now and cling to it. Have faith in something, even if that something is yourself. And when the moment comes to test your mettle, break out the picture of your daughter, the letter from your wife, the cross pendent, or just close your eyes for a moment and remember. And then unleash the hope within. It is at that moment that you will do great and impossible things.

In the words of Napoleon Bonaparte, "Courage is like love; it must have hope for nourishment."

PRINCIPLES OF SELF DEFENSE

Hands aren't easily pried open. It is better to avoid the grip than to escape it.

Once your attacker has his hands on you, there are a few options for you to choose from, depending on where he grabs you and how he grabs you. Say for instance, someone grabs your wrist to drag you off. You can simply pull your arm toward the weak side of his grip, called the gate (where his thumb meets his index finger). It's usually that simple, but in my self-defense classes I always teach the "circle out" method, which is more effective at defeating the grip of a stronger opponent. Of course, this method would not work for a very strong two-handed grab on one wrist, or a lapel grab. Unfortunately, martial arts instructors everywhere are teaching that to escape a lapel (or shirt) grab, all you have to do is reach across both attacker's hands with your right hand, grab the pinky side of your attacker's right hand (which is peacefully resting on your left chest), then peel the hand away, which results in the perfect set-up for you to break his arm at the elbow, then apply a takedown to your opponent who is still very docile, despite all you've done to him. But no matter how many "experts" teach it, that method just doesn't go the way you learn and practice it.

The frightening truth is, your attacker will not be that submissive. If someone grabs your shirt, it's for a reason. Usually it's to get your attention, or to change your location to one of his choosing. He won't just stand there waiting for you to defend yourself. Also, more than likely his grip will be very tight and very difficult to open once it is locked onto your appendage or article of clothing. Therefore, it is far easier and more effective to avoid your attacker's grip than to attempt to pry it off you.

To avoid being grabbed by someone you don't trust, you should block his hands with yours as they come near you to grab. I teach some very basic blocking techniques in my self-defense classes, which I will share with you here. While similar to the blocks found in many martial arts styles, the following blocks are performed without a set starting point, middle point, or path to the end point. It is important to try to block with your forearm, because it is a broader surface than your hand and is not as easily missed. Also, your hand has many small bones which are fragile and can be injured very easily. Your forearm, not so much. In order to block with your forearm instead of your hand, timing is very important. You must practice blocking to meet his hand with your arm at just the right time. Without practice, you will block too soon or too late, both of which will end up badly for you.

In order to block an incoming grab or widely arcing punch toward your head, raise your hand about forehead level and reach toward the attacker's arm. It is easier to block an attack on your left side with your left hand, and an attack on your right side with your right hand. However, it doesn't matter what side you use; the most important part is making sure the attack does not succeed.

To block a punch coming straight at your face (like a boxer's jab or cross), simply swat your aggressor's fist away from your face as it comes near. Don't close your eyes in anticipation of the pain, but keep them open and watch your timing and distance. Again, it is easier to match sides so that you can push the fist down and across the body, but whatever works. There are no rules here.

Circle out and open the gate.

If your attacker is able to get his hands on your wrists, forearms, or even your upper arm, the response is quite simple, circle out. As described above, you could simply jerk your appendage toward the gate of the attacker's grip, but this can often fail, especially if your attacker has you by the elbow or upper arm with an extremely strong grasp. The circle out method has a much greater rate of success regardless of what part of the arm the opponent has a grasp on. For added effectiveness in case of that extremely strong grasp, clasp your hands and quickly circle out using the strength of both arms. The circle out also works very well to defeat the grip before it is even established.

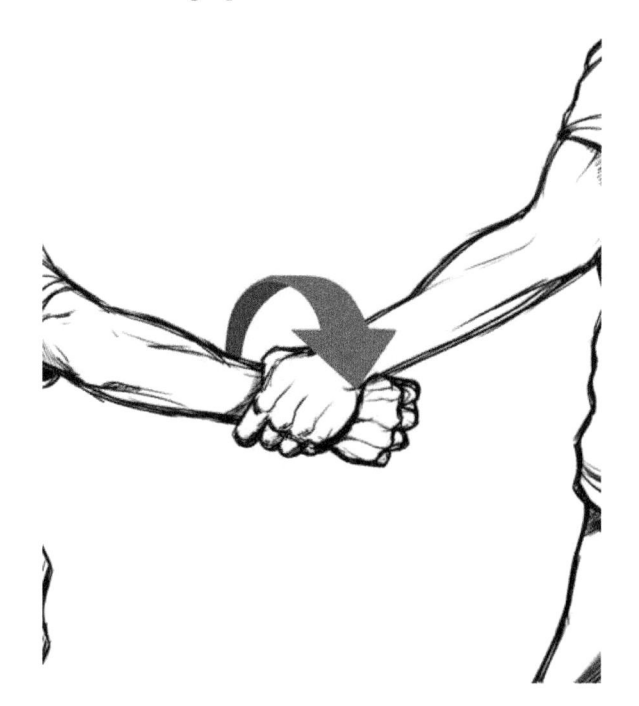

Every joint has a limit.

Joints are very complex parts of the human body that are made up of many smaller parts that combine to provide movement. Injury to a joint can hinder that movement and cause a great deal of pain. Knowing the limits of a joint allows you to push those limits with your attacker's joints, causing severe pain and if you continue to push the joint past its limit, damage to the components of the joint can occur. Consequentially your attacker will not be able to use the joint and may halt his attack due to the pain, allowing you to escape. There are eight sets of moving joints in the human body which I will focus on that can be used to your advantage: the neck, shoulders, elbows, wrists, fingers, knees, ankles, and toes (the hips are a major set of joints that can also be manipulated, but I will not cover those techniques here due to the difficulty of those techniques). These junctions all fall into categories or types that help describe their function. But first, in order to know the limits of each joint, it helps to know how it operates.

The neck is a **pivot point** which allows limited rotating movements. That means that pushing or twisting the neck to its limit can be easier than many other joints. However, because the neck consists of a portion of the spine, it is very dangerous to manipulate it, even in practice. Use extreme caution and only perform techniques on the neck joints under the watchful eye of a qualified instructor.

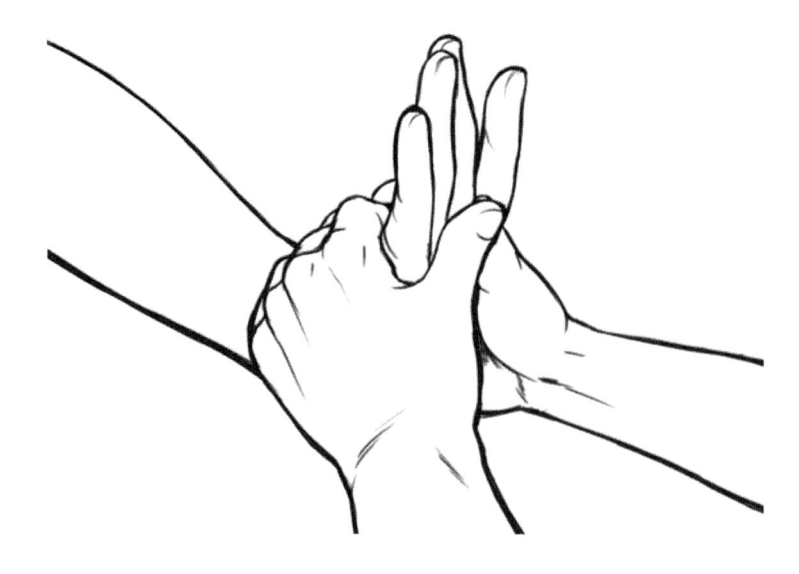

Regardless of the Hollywood hype, twisting a person's head sideways doesn't kill them, unless you apply a hard-core amount of leverage and strength to basically make them face about 157 degrees to their rear (5 o'clock). However, a much more effective method of injuring an assailant would be to force the neck to bend (rather than turn) further than intended. This can be easily accomplished by grasping the head and pulling it down sideways until the ear touches the shoulder, forward until the chin touches the chest, or (most effective – and dangerous!) backward until… well, you will know it when your attacker hits the ground. Let me remind you that practicing neck cranks and manipulations are extremely dangerous and should not be performed haphazardly. Please seek professional instruction before attempting to experiment with these types of methods!

Ball and socket joints

Such as the shoulder and hip joints, allow movement in many different directions including forward, backward, sideways, and even rotating motions. Because of the thicker bones, cartilage, ligaments and tendons surrounding these ball and socket joints, as well as their inherently flexible nature, it can be quite difficult to find limits to these joints. However, they all have limits, and with some training you can learn to push them to and past their breaking point if the need arises.

There are methods of dislocating someone's shoulders, but they require conditions which are infrequently met, and even then a fairly high amount of strength and knowledge about the anatomy of a shoulder. However, it is far easier to cause damage to a rotator cuff, which is the group of muscles and tendons that surround the shoulder joint. The rotator cuff can become injured when the person reaches upward and too far backward. This can be accomplished by pushing his elbow over his shoulder and back behind him. Another way of causing significant pain is by wrenching the arm underneath the shoulder and behind the back, pulling the hand up the center of the back until you reach a breaking point. While this is pretty common, it hurts the shoulder but requires a lot of strength to reach the breaking point. You are essentially fighting your attacker's entire set of chest, arm, and back muscles using just your arm muscles if you both are standing (it's even more difficult to perform while wrestling on the ground).

Hinge joints

Such as the fingers, knees, elbows, and toes, allow only bending and straightening movements. These are generally the easiest to defeat, because they only bend forward and backward and usually have limits to just how far forward and backward they can go without injury. Fingers are the easiest to manipulate because of their small breadth and relative length; they are fairly easy to grasp and very easy to bend beyond the breaking point. Toes are the next easiest, but are usually covered by shoes. Elbows are easily broken by holding the wrist stationary while striking at or near the elbow in a manner that does not allow the attacker to move his torso to compensate for his wrist's immovable position. When done quickly and with enough force, the elbow will hyperextend and cause significant injury to the assailant. Knees, because of the size of the structuring of the legs and the muscles involved, are the most difficult of the hinge joints to hyperextend. However, it isn't impossible with the right leverage.

Gliding joints (also known as ellipsoidal joints)

Allow all types of movements except for pivoting. The wrist is a gliding joint, as is the ankle. Depending on the size of the person and the muscular makeup in his arms, the wrist can be very easy to bend, or it can be relatively difficult. And, although some wrists are very flexible and can bend fully forward and backward,

SELF-DEFENSE BASICS

nearly all wrists will sustain a painful injury if bent sideways. Although attempting to force a very muscular person's wrist to bend sideways is more difficult than bending it forward or backward, it can be done with proper leverage, and it generally causes pain more instantaneously than the alternative. Also, since the wrist is not meant to pivot, forcing it to do so will also cause damage to the joint.

The ankle is another relatively strong joint due to the muscles which help support it. However, it can be used to disable your attacker. Because, as the saying goes, if you cannot stand, you cannot fight. More accurately, if your attacker cannot stand, he cannot chase you while you escape.

In order to hyperextend the ankle, your attacker should be placed on his back using whatever method works best for you. Grab one foot and hold it securely under one of your arms. Tuck it high into your armpit, making sure to focus on the foot itself, not the leg. With the opponent still on the ground face up, quickly lie back and hold onto the foot. This will undoubtedly cause a great deal of pain for your attacker, and it may or may not injure him, depending on the muscular makeup of his ankle. You can add a dash of pain by simply arching your back and hugging his foot tightly. If he isn't triple-jointed or numb from drugs, your attacker should be crying his apologies to you in the key of high C by now.

Your attacker will give you the tools to use against him.

It isn't often you hear a positive statement in regards to being attacked. But there is a silver lining. Every time your attacker touches you, if even for an instant, he is giving you something that you can use to defeat him. When he grabs, shoves, pulls, or punches you, he essentially hands you his entire arm. All you have to do is reach out and take it. The same goes for when he kicks you. His leg and foot become yours, as soon as you grab it. If he tackles you, he has just said to you, "Here is my body; do with it what you may."

The trick here is speed and timing. You must learn to respond to the presentation of a person's limbs within close proximity to your body. Just as you practice blocking (which is still more effective for survival purposes), you must also practice basic grappling techniques.

An example to this principle is a response to a shove. Practice this in slow motion before moving on to higher speed applications, and please be careful with your training partner's wrist – this puts a lot of strain on that and other joints. Your opponent shoves you with one or both hands. While his hands are still on your chest, trap them and keep them pinned to your chest. Allow his shove to push you back one step (only one foot moves; the other remains firmly planted in place), and then turn your body in the direction of the foot you moved. If your opponent used both hands to shove you, it doesn't matter which way you turn as long as you trapped both hands tightly. If you've only trapped one hand (let's say for instance you trapped his right hand), you should pivot clockwise. Step back with your right foot and turn to your right. Move your entire body as one unit, hips and shoulders together. If you've trapped his left hand, then you should turn counter clockwise. Step back with your left foot and turn to your left. In this manner, your attacker will be facing in the same direction as you, and you can use his entire arm which he has just provided to you against him. A slight bend at the waist at the end of your rotation should bring him to his knees. Release and escape. You're welcome.

Keep your power close to your heart.

This principle is best explained by experience. Find a 5 pound weight, or maybe a gallon of milk to lift. First try to lift the object from a distance. Keep your arms straight in front of you and lift using only your arm muscles. It's very difficult, isn't it? Now lift the same object while keeping it close to your body.

Lift with all the muscles you need to use. You will notice how much easier it is to lift the item when it is closer to you than it is when it is far away. The difference is in muscle groups. You are using only forearm and side muscles at a distance, but when you bring the item close to your body, you use your biceps, triceps, pectorals, core and shoulder muscles together, which is more efficient at applying upward pressure to your object. Similarly, when you perform a technique such as a wrist lock or arm bar, you should keep your hands close to your chest in order to maximize the effort of your muscle groups. A mistake I see almost all students make when learning the wristlock and standing arm bar techniques is pushing the opponent's whole hand away from the body. This places the assailant's arm outside your "power zone" and inside his, which will allow him to easily defeat your grip and counterattack. So remember, keep your power close to your heart. Pull it in close like you intend to hug it, and you will have much more power to exert on your attacker.

Economy of Motion.

Every move you make in a combat situation should be performed with efficiency, directness, and simplicity. Any movement that does not have a direct effect on the opponent in your favor is wasted movement. Remember: the shortest distance between two points is a straight line. That means that your hands should follow a straight line from their resting point to the target in order to reach the target in the shortest amount of time. This will result not only in faster strikes, but also reduced fatigue because you are not wasting energy "chambering" your strike, and, if your hands are kept in a defensive position before the strike, more powerful strikes because you will be striking from your power zone as mentioned above in "Keep your power close to your heart".

Economy of motion also includes simplicity of technique. We have already discussed how survival stress affects fine and complex motor skills. We know that when your heart rate reaches 145 beats per minute, that advanced black belt move where you lift the opponent's arm, step under in a cross-legged stance, strike his ribs with a glancing elbow, allow his forward motion of doubling over assist you in placing him into a standing arm bar (because he is definitely reeling from the pain of that glancing elbow!), then step behind your opponent, twisting his arm up overhead and taking him to the ground while applying a standing full body arm bar and simultaneous wristlock, won't work. Try as you might, if you are in hard core, fight or flight survival mode, your brain will not allow you to perform complex movements like those, because it "knows" instinctively that those kinds of techniques have a high chance of failure. Bottom line, simple is better.

Combining movements is also economical. That is why I teach what is known as "bursting" – blocking your attacker's strikes while counterattacking at the same time. This allows no time for your assailant to perform follow-up strikes and places you in a position of advantage. It takes a lot of practice to program your mind and body to instinctively block and strike simultaneously, but once it's learned it becomes second nature. Your friends and family will inevitably hate your newfound skill, because all who attempt to startle you for fun will end up being punched! I have been known to punch people who wake me up too abruptly. I don't choose to do it; my reflexes take over and my body reacts to the chaos it perceives. While it may seem brutal, it is very comforting to know that your body can act first without your thoughts interfering. One caveat to that involves where to keep weapons, specifically firearms. I personally can't sleep with a handgun under my pillow or in a bedside holster, because I am the most likely of all the people I know to wake up shooting at the noise I have not identified yet. So for my family's safety I choose to place my handguns just out of reach but readily accessible nonetheless.

Where the head goes the body follows.

This mantra has been used in a multitude of applications: martial arts, ballet, football – even psychology and philosophy! If you haven't noticed, we humans move a little differently from four-legged animals; while normal movement involves four legs for them, we only use two. That means that our balance is more fragile and easily disrupted. It is said that our center of gravity, or center of balance is in the trunk, that is, the pelvis. And that's true. Notice that when you stand in one place, especially on one leg, your hips are naturally over your foot. If you attempt to move your hips from over your foot, you will lose balance. Likewise while standing on both feet your hips are naturally centered over the feet. You may spread your feet further than shoulder width apart, but your hips will remain at the center point between and above them. But move your hips forward or backward and you will fall. Your balance will remain intact for as long as your hips are above your feet.

While the pelvis is most assuredly the center of balance in humans, it can be quite difficult to grab a rather large attacker by his massive hips and move him. However, what can be much more effective is grabbing him by his head and moving him.

Regardless of where the center of gravity is, the "head bone" is still, after all these years, connected to the spine which leads directly to the hip bone. It's like there's a large handle that we can grab and simply "unmake" our aggressor's balance!

In my self-defense classes I don't teach people to punch their attackers; instead I teach an open-hand strike to the chin, and then I augment that technique with a continual push through. In other words, when facing an opponent, push his chin upward and backward, so that he first looks to the sky, and then his head is pushed backwards. If you follow through and move with your attacker you can push him faster than he can back-step, which will result in his head going back past his hips – his center of gravity. And we all know what happens then. Mister Aggressor loses his balance and falls back, giving you the perfect opportunity to run for the door!

One of my very favorite techniques involving the head is one used by bodyguards and executive protection agents everywhere. Instead of simply shoving the threat backwards, they will grab the head with both hands and twist, while leading it downward in front or behind them. It takes them literally less than a second to neutralize a threat and it works almost every time!

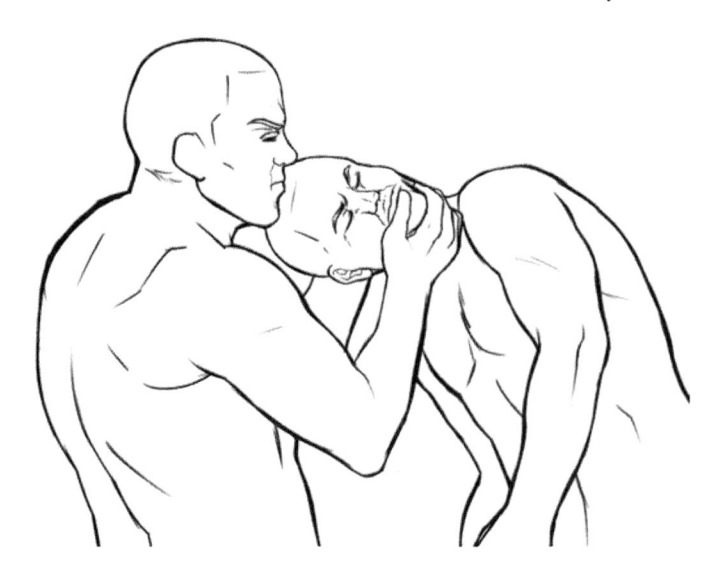

Do not rely on pain compliance; physically move your opponent.

There are literally hundreds of self-defense programs out there, some for military and law enforcement, and some marketed toward civilians. Nearly all of them have one thing in common: pain compliance. Pain compliance is simply the use of pain to make your enemy submit and give up. There are many problems with this method, however. Firstly, not everyone feels pain the same way, and not everyone reacts the same to it. I know people who break down and cry when they feel a substantial amount of pain, and I know others who get angry. There are people who, upon reaching a certain threshold, will faint, and others who will go berserk and attack with even greater ferocity.

One of my original Karate instructors was a high school classmate named James Glass. He was very large even as a teenager, and he was highly skilled in his martial arts, arguably more so than the other instructors at that dojo. He worked out a lot and he walked everywhere he went, so he was in shape. And when I say James was in shape, I mean to look at him conjured thoughts of military tanks!

What was truly amazing about James Glass was that he didn't seem to feel pain. I know that is scientifically inaccurate – everyone feels pain. But James didn't respond to it at all! We had a guest instructor visit the dojo one day and teach us about pressure points.

For those of you who do not know what pressure points are, take a finger and press on your forearm; anywhere will do. Press harder. Doesn't really hurt much, does it? Now take the same finger and press just behind your jaw hinge, underneath your ear. Press in and slightly forward toward your face. That is a pressure point – one of hundreds (some say thousands) of points on your body which are sensitive to pressure. These points, when pressed or struck, cause significant pain or disruption in the body or some portion of it.

So, this guest instructor began demonstrating on multiple students how effective the techniques of his martial art style were. One by one they dropped, stepped back, or yelled in agony. That is, until he reached James. James stood there with a puzzled look on his face as if to suggest he wasn't aware that he was being touched. Equally confused was the guest instructor who was unable to make James move or yell. He wrote it off at first, probably to avoid embarrassment, and moved on to the next pressure point. After the entire line of students "tapped" or yelled from the pain, he again approached James Glass. Pressing on the chosen pressure point, James just shrugged. It wasn't that James was being difficult; he just wasn't feeling anything unusual. The guest instructor was so intrigued by James's resistance to his pressure points, that he actually dismissed all the other students and began poking around on James exclusively. For the next three to five minutes, he pressed on about thirty points, eliciting nothing more than a raised eyebrow from James.

Through the years I've hit a few people and been hit by a few. What I have noticed, aside from some people's extraordinary tolerance to pain, is that larger and more muscular people are less susceptible to the effects of certain pressure points. I believe this to be because the layer of muscle (or fat in some cases) covers up and protects the sensitive nerves that comprise the pressure point, making them difficult to strike in a fight. Although some points actually disrupt the use of limbs rather than just inciting pain, most of them enjoy the same protection from the muscles as do all the others (with a few exceptions). Regardless of the reason, it is safe to say that relying on pain compliance is not an effective method. A much better way of controlling your assailant is by enacting a physical change in his position. Grab his head and move him, use his arm to bring him down, or apply a throw or takedown – whatever you do, don't rely on him to give in because of pain; he may not be so inclined.

Don't resist a force greater than you; use your attacker's force and direction against him.

Newton's first law of motion (often referred to as the law of inertia) states that an object at rest stays at rest and an object in motion stays in motion with the same speed and in the same direction unless acted upon by an *unbalanced force*. What that means is that if your attacker, weighing about 185 pounds, lunges toward you to tackle you, and you weigh only 145 pounds, there are two objects in play – your attacker who is in motion, and you who are at rest. An object in motion (your attacker) will remain in motion with the same speed and in the same direction until he collides with you. Because you are at rest, you will exert a small force against the attacker, but not enough to stop him dead in his tracks. You will, however, slow him down enough for gravity to take over. That will result in him tackling you to the ground and landing squarely on top of you unless some other event causes him to land elsewhere. Had you both weighed the same, you could theoretically exert a similar amount of force to counteract your attacker's force, which would result in more of a stalemate. However, that is an ideal which almost never happens in reality.

Meeting a heavier opponent force-against-force is almost never a good idea. If your assailant attempts a tackle or other full-body attack, it is in your best interest to either redirect the attack, or use the attacker's force and direction against him. It takes practice and good timing (where have we heard *that* before?), but once you have it down, it could save your life.

To redirect a full-body attack, simply step off the line of attack and shove or shoulder-butt the enemy sideways as he comes into range. This will be very difficult to do if he is able to grab you before the shove. The usual result is an unbalanced attacker falling face first in front of you, which will allow you a few seconds to run away.

To use the attacker's force and direction against him, you must first allow him to get within very close range, and then, instead of redirecting him to another direction, you will reposition yourself to the side and "help" him continue his forward momentum. The result is very similar to the redirect approach, but because you have helped your attacker to maintain his direction, his speed actually increases a little bit. This will not be expected, and will catch him off guard as he had intended to slow down upon impact with your body. Instead he will probably fall uncontrollably to the floor somewhat dazed. His confusion and surprise can work to your advantage, but run quickly, because it won't last long.

Close the gap and overwhelm your attacker.

It's one of my biggest pet peeves: I go to a martial arts seminar or self-defense class, and there is the instructor, all professional and confident in himself and his abilities. And he begins to teach. He shows his techniques on an "opponent" which stands perfectly still as he grabs the instructor almost lifelessly. There is no attack; there is no realism; there's not even any acting like the opponent means business. Sure, that's great for the first couple of practice repetitions, but after that a student should be allowed to progress and get better at the technique in real time, with some degree of resistance (safely, of course). Without resistance, the practitioner cannot possibly know whether the technique actually works, or if it is just something a computer nerd sat and thought of while playing around with his Power Ranger action figures! And without some realistic resistance, the student will never muster the courage to get into the fight and do what needs to be done, because fear will most certainly take over. Remember, survival stress will not allow you to perform an action that your subconscious does not have enough confidence in. Survival mode takes over and will make you freeze up – that's the dark side of the "fight-or-flight" mechanism.

There's a reason the drill sergeants at Fort Benning beat the boots off of us during Modern Army Combatives training; had they not added a touch of realism (along with the safety of mouth guards, boxing gloves, and other regulations), we may never have known just what it takes to fight through and overcome, to "close the gap" and finish the fight. It was a great training and confidence building exercise that I will never forget.

The clinch drill I performed in Basic Training also helped me to realize how many times I had failed to rush in and finish the fight. How many times had I stood from afar, just out of reach of my opponent, be it in a sanctioned tournament, or a street fight? How many times had I taken the "safe" route of analyzing my opponent's body language, so that I could play a careful game of full-contact chess, rather than closing the gap and finishing the fight? I'd say far too many.

In a real, down-and-dirty, life on the line fight, you gotta get in there. You gotta close the gap between you and the person who wants to control you, and maybe wants you dead. You can't sit back and wait; you don't have time. Remember, 10 to 15 seconds goes fast when you're winning, but it lasts a lifetime when you're losing. Get in there; close the gap, overwhelm your attacker with violence of action. Use speed, strength, surprise, and all-out aggression to achieve total dominance over your attacker. Fight like your life depends on it – because it does!

An injured dog bites the hardest.

Hollywood strikes again! I'm done watching action movies that aren't directed by someone who knows about combat. It's another of my pet peeves: the bad guys saturate the air with bullets and nobody gets hurt; stuff blows up as soon as a bullet touches it, and the good guys fling a round down range and instantly the bad guy is dead. Truth is it's become one of our expectations. You shoot someone anywhere in the torso or head and you can rest easy because the bad guy has been shot; he's dead! But that's not how it works in real life. Sure, you can die from gunshot wounds – it happens all the time. But it's rarely instantaneous. It takes time to bleed out from one little hole, or even ten, even if you are shot in the heart or lung. You can certainly die instantly from a gunshot to the head, *if* it hits the right spot (or if the bullet comes from a high-powered rifle). But there are plenty of cases that show that people can survive even a head shot at close range.

I say all that to emphasize the importance of persistence. If you are in a fight for your life, don't believe the Hollywood hype; just because you are injured does not mean you can't fight and survive. Just because you are shot, even multiple times, does not mean you can't overcome and survive. Just because you feel like you're dying does not mean you will. Get through it. Summon the need-to, and do what needs to be done. You *will* survive.

SELF-DEFENSE BASICS

Always cheat. Always win.

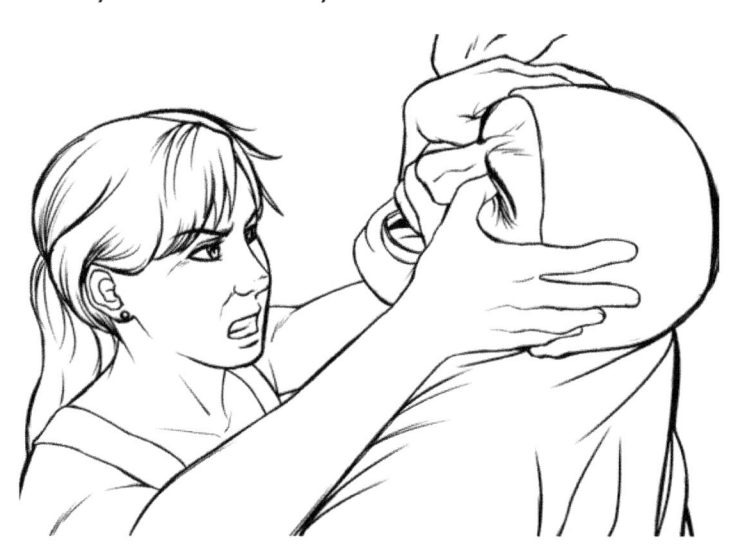

It's time for another reality check. I know that most of us have been taught since infancy that cheaters never win and winners never cheat. And while that may be true in board games and sports, the rules of combat are infinitely different. When your life is on the line, the only thing that matters is surviving. What you do to survive, save for a few extreme examples, doesn't matter much. Biting may have gotten Mike expelled from the boxing ring, but if that's what you have to do to survive a deadly encounter with a rapist or what have you, then so be it. Clawing at someone's face may not be how you play well with others, but in a real fight, break out the press-ons and start clawing! If you're frustrated because your Karate instructor won't let you kick your opponent in the balls (let's be blunt, shall we?), fear not, because those rules don't apply on the street!

There are a few things to consider before you go and buy yourself an Uzi to bring to your next bar fight. You should definitely know the laws in the United States, the laws in your state, and also the laws in your municipality, your city, and your county. You can usually find this information online, but the best place to learn it will be from an attorney who specializes in criminal law. While asking a police officer can shed some insight into what you want to know, most cops are not legal experts and can lead you astray with their interpretations of the laws. No offense to the police– thanks for your service to your community! You will most likely find it illegal to shoot someone who isn't posing a pretty significant threat to your life, regardless of the threatening words. Consult with a legal expert just to be sure you understand your legal and moral boundaries. You should definitely do that now, that is, sooner before later.

Don't turn your back.

I was already ahead by four points. I was beaming with pride, because I had already earned first place with my kata (form), and I was most assuredly going to take first place in sparring as well. My entire dojo including all the instructors were watching and cheering me on. My opponent seemed relaxed, but my tension was way up. Never before had I gotten first place in both events in one meet, and I was one point from doing just that. The judge called "hajime" (pronounced ha-gee-*may*, which means "begin"), and I quickly and expertly delivered a beautiful side kick into my opponent's ribs. In the rules of the Mississippi Karate Association at the time, a kick to the side or front torso counted as two points. However, a kick below the waist would not count, and would cost you a point the second time, as would a strike after the call of "yame" (pronounced ya-*may*, meaning "stop"). The lead judge called "yame", and just a microsecond later, my opponent dropped down into a front stance and kicked me hard between the legs. And then he turned his back to walk away. I did not think about anything; I didn't decide to pursue him, it was just instinct. He kicked me with an obvious intent to cause bodily harm, and my warrior instinct took the wheel and I went after him. I was stopped in my tracks by a very large black-belt judge who saw it coming. Once I stopped long enough to think, I felt the effects of that kick. I won the match due to the last two points I earned with my kick and the point awarded to me for striking after the call, but I could not walk the next day – at all.

There are two takeaways to this narrative, the first being that kicking a man in his nether regions does not always stop him like a brick wall. In the heat of battle, some men can take that hit and keep going, succumbing to it later, if at all. The second lesson to be learned is, do not assume the fight is over just because it should be. As mentioned a couple of sections ago (an injured dog bites the hardest), just because you are injured does not mean you can't continue. Likewise, just because you injure your enemy does not mean that the fight is over. Run if you can, but don't underestimate the ability of humans to act like wolves and pursue their prey. That mistake can be deadly.

LESSON 5

WEAPONS

At work, I carry a firearm because I am head of security for a large corporation. However, I know that even when I am not at work, there are bad people seeking to harm innocents. Otherwise there would be no need for the existence of my job, or this book for that matter. Therefore I choose to carry concealed when I'm not at work. I almost always have a handgun on me or within close reach – even while I am at home. There have been many home invasion cases on the news, and I know that in a violent situation there will be no time to run to another room and grab a weapon.

Furthermore, I also keep a knife handy, just in case I'm not able to use my firearm. Backup guns are heavy (even when they're light), and a knife can be a useful tool for tasks other than self-defense. I can't imagine how often I've used my knife to do small tasks like cutting a box or string etc. Heck, I've even washed off my blade and used it to cut food! As versatile as knives are, it is my opinion that all gentlemen and most ladies should keep a pocket knife with them when they are away from home.

And when the going gets really tough, there are many blunt force weapons to be found all around you: a stapler, broom stick or chair; all these things can be picked up and used to hit the attacker. Any hard object that you can easily pick up and swing quickly will do.

In this lesson I will teach you how to effectively use these weapons, as well as how to defend against them. As usual, these techniques are very dangerous, even in practice, and should not be performed without the careful guidance of a qualified self-defense instructor.

FIREARMS

If you reside in or frequent a state which allows firearms, and you can legally own and carry one, you should definitely consider doing so. However, before picking up a deadly weapon, it would be best to learn firearm safety. I will touch on the subject here, but it is no substitute for in-person training by a qualified instructor. Firearm safety can't be simply read; it is a discipline which takes time and practice to learn, just like martial arts and the principles within this book.

Firearm Safety

According to the National Rifle Association, the foremost authority on firearm safety and usage, there are three fundamental safety rules which every gun handler should always follow…all the time.

1 **Always point the gun in a safe direction.** Another way of stating this is, never point a gun at anything you are not willing to *destroy*. This primary rule of gun safety ensures a firearm will not harm you or others when discharged. Never trust that the safety device(s) of the gun will work. Mechanical devices sometimes fail. Trust me; I've seen it happen *twice*. The saving grace in both incidents was that both times the gun was pointed in a safe direction when it fired. When outdoors, point the gun toward the ground or towards the

target. If you are indoors, be mindful that a bullet can penetrate ceilings, floors, walls, windows, and doors. Remember where other people are and don't point in their direction.

2 **Keep your finger off the trigger until ready to shoot.** When holding a gun, rest your finger on the trigger guard or along the side of the gun. Do not touch the trigger unless you are ready to pull it.

3 **Keep the gun unloaded until ready to use.** Immediately engage the safety device, remove the magazine, open the action and check the chamber when you pick up a gun.

What kind of gun should I get?

As much as I would enjoy running down a list of every firearm I think every American should own, I will stick to wisdom and simplicity concerning your choice of firearms. The truth is, which firearm(s) you choose depends specifically on what you intend to use it for, what your priorities and preferred features are in a gun, and who will be using it. Ok, so now you are even more confused than ever. Right? Well, don't sweat it; I'm going to explain just what you need to know, and I'm gonna try to keep it interesting. Ok? Alright, here goes!

The kind of gun you choose will depend greatly on its purpose. Will you be wanting a home defense gun for defending your home in the middle of the night, a concealed carry gun for taking with you everywhere you go, or an open carry for out-in-town carry? I'm specifying only those guns which you would use for defensive purposes, because that is the main focus of this book. However, there are plenty of other guns you can get for hunting, plinking, and sport shooting which are not designed for tactical and defensive use, but still sling lead just as well as those made for self-defense.

For home defense, many people prefer a shotgun. In case you aren't familiar with shotguns, they are relatively long guns which

SELF PROTECTION

fire shot shells – large diameter plastic shells loaded with multiple bullet-sized projectiles, or "shot". When fired, all the projectiles are expelled at the same time, spreading out and covering a larger area instead of concentrating on a pinpoint accurate target. The longer the distance from the end of the barrel, the wider the spread, and the lower the velocity, which means less effectiveness at medium range and almost no effect at long range (past 50 yards).The good side to this is, you don't have to be extremely accurate with a shotgun at the close distances found in most homes, just point and shoot. The bad side, however, is that every pellet that doesn't hit your intended target must end up somewhere. Let's hope it isn't an innocent bystander or loved one. Also, the recoil (commonly referred to as "kick") of many shotguns is more than some people can handle. 12 gauge is a very popular caliber, because it essentially throws nine .33 caliber bullets from a single 00-buck (also known as "double-ought buckshot") cartridge, carrying with them a sledgehammer worth of energy, and delivering a similar sledgehammer worth of kick to your shoulder. My personal favorite shotgun is the Mossberg 500 series, because it is simple to operate, simple to maintain, and fairly inexpensive. For you bargain hunters out there, some manufacturers offer a tactical 12 gauge shotgun for less than you would pay for a basic Mossberg, and the specs are nearly identical.

Another option for home defense, specifically for someone who doesn't weigh enough to stand up to the massive recoil some shotguns produce, is an AR-15. The "Armalite Rifle" (commonly mistaken to be an assault rifle due to the "AR" in its name) is usually chambered in .223 Remington, which is *nearly* synonymous with the 5.56 NATO round. Many AR-15's can hold both calibers, while some can only be loaded with .223 ammunition. This is an aggressive looking rifle which easily conjures images of U.S. military and law enforcement S.W.A.T. teams on full assault. Despite the vicious image, it fires a much smaller projectile than the 12 gauge shotgun, but it certainly holds its own. While one can't compare a .223/5.56 round to a 12 gauge in terms of energy transfer (what most people mistakenly call "stopping power"), the AR holds a special place in home defense, especially if you get a short-barrel configuration similar to an M4. The down side to the AR is its bad boy image (if that can be considered a negative), and at the time of this writing the rifle costs between $900 and $3000, depending on quality and branding. Additionally, if you are anything like me, you will buy one with the intention of simply using it for home defense, and then end up spending a house note or two on modifications and accessories, because the AR is such a modular weapon, it just begs for upgrades!

I personally don't feel the need for a shotgun, a rifle, and a handgun for home defense; instead I have opted to keep my duty weapon handy at all times. If you are able to own a defensive handgun in your home, you may want a large frame, full size handgun because of many factors. First, most of the larger handguns weigh more and therefore they "kick" less.

Secondly, a larger frame equals more gripping space for when you are holding, firing, loading and reloading the weapon. When you are under stress, it will already be more difficult to perform those reloading actions, so you shouldn't further complicate the process with tiny handgun parts and pieces.

The third reason (and my favorite excuse to keep a full size handgun around) is the psychological factor. Not only does it feel great to grab a hand cannon when you feel like your life is in danger, but the bad guy reacts differently as well. According to "*Handgun Wounding Factors and Effectiveness*", an FBI training material,

"Psychological factors are probably the most important relative to achieving rapid incapacitation from a gunshot wound to the torso. Awareness of the injury (often delayed by the suppression of pain); fear of injury, death, blood or pain;

SELF PROTECTION

intimidation by the weapon or the act of being shot; preconceived notions of what people do when they are shot; or the simple desire to quit can all lead to incapacitation even from minor wounds." – Special Agent Urey W. Patrick of the FBI Firearms Training Unit (emphasis added).

I've never been a fan of revolvers, mainly because they hold such a limited amount of ammunition (usually five or six rounds), and reloading is a hassle in comparison to the alternative. However, revolvers launch lead too, and they may fit your hands better and they are easier to operate for most people. Another thing in favor of revolvers is that they rarely malfunction. Semiautos can "jam" if dirt or lint gets in the slide, if any of the springs get weak, if the magazine is of poor quality, or if your grip isn't stable enough. But as long as there is ammo in a revolver, just pull the trigger and it will go "bang". I'd say that's a big argument in the wheel gun's favor.

I'm swallowing a huge chunk of my pride as I write this paragraph, because a friend of mine and I have argued the statistics and specs of the .45 ACP against other, smaller rounds for over a year, and I have always maintained what I was taught by the old dogs – that you never attend a gunfight with a handgun, the caliber of which does not start with a "4". While I once maintained that the .45 Automatic Colt Pistol (ACP) is the most perfect pistol cartridge, the truth is in the ballistics. It appears that in terms of energy transfer a .357 Magnum is a better round, though only marginally. While the .45, a bullet made specifically for semi-automatic handguns, is indeed an awesome caliber when it comes to so-called stopping power (which is a myth), doling out 494 ft-lbs of energy with a 200-grain bullet, the .357 Magnum, which is a revolver-only caliber, dishes it out at roughly 600 ft-lbs! What that means is that both the .357 Magnum and .45 ACP are both heavy and slow in comparison with many other handgun bullets, which translates into all their energy being dumped into the bad guy, assuming that you shoot him squarely in his torso instead of an arm or leg. The takeaway to this is, if you want a semi-automatic weapon, you just about can't go wrong with a .45 ACP. And if you prefer a revolver because you think you can't operate the slide on a semi-auto (or for whatever reason), the .357 Magnum will do the trick. If you absolutely must use smaller calibers, I would advise you to stick to .40 Smith & Wesson for semiauto guns and .38 Special for revolver, and nothing less.

Should you be so blessed as to live in a state and have the moral propensity to carry a concealed weapon outside your home (legally, of course), you will more likely want a small frame handgun. Of course I love my Sig Sauer model 1911 .45 ACP, semiautomatic handgun. However, the advantage of carrying a lightweight, unobtrusive handgun for hours at a time and forgetting that it's there is priceless. Additionally, being able to conceal *and fire* a gun from inside your pocket or purse without worrying about the slide's necessity to function and chamber another round outweighs my wish to carry three more rounds in the magazine. It is for those reasons that some people like small or medium sized revolvers, specifically the "snub-nose" ones with 2-inch barrels.

I bought my first revolver from my mother-in-law just a couple of months ago, and after changing the plastic stock grips to soft rubber grips, I love it. Even though it's a "measly" .38 Special (which is not that measly a bullet) that only holds five rounds, I can't help but feel safe with it in my vehicle or holstered and tucked neatly inside my waist band when I'm not carrying my bulky 1911. No, it's not exactly a .357 Magnum, and it's not my beloved .45 ACP, but it's small enough to be comfortably concealed, yet powerful enough to make the bad guy get off me. And at the end of the day, that's all that really matters. If you do decide to carry a revolver, Smith & Wesson makes a great line of revolvers; I'd even venture to say they are the leaders in the defensive revolver market (that's not paid advertising; that's my honest opinion). For concealed carry purposes I suggest getting a hammerless model – a revolver that has no external hammer – because hammers have a tendency to hook on to pockets, purses, and clothing.

Defense against a handgun

Preparing to defend yourself against a firearm could be the scariest moment of your life. Seeing the gun pointed at you and knowing that it could go off, even if accidentally, rightfully strikes fear into most people. My recommendation is that if at all possible, do not attempt to fight someone who is threatening you with a gun; if all they want is money or valuables, simply give them what they want. Your possessions are not worth your life.

However, if your attacker clearly wants more, if he obviously plans to kill you or someone else, or if he plans to kidnap you or take a hostage, you may consider fighting back as a last resort to save your life. In case that becomes a reality, your attacker will need to be close in order to effectively defend yourself against him. Think arm's length or closer. If there is distance between you,

WEAPONS

consider running, as long as you think you can make it. If you are able to run, do so in a zig-zag pattern to make it difficult to aim at you. Don't just run a couple of steps and then turn; run for two full seconds in one direction, and then turn and run for two full seconds in the opposite direction. Continue to zig-zag until you are behind cover, or until your attacker is no longer a threat.

To defend against a handgun within arm's reach:

1 **Expect the gun to go "boom!"** As soon as you touch it, the gun will probably fire. You need to expect the "boom" and it's going to be loud as hell, but you have to ignore the boom at all costs in order to follow through and finish the fight.

2 **Get off the line of attack and close the gap.** I can't emphasize enough, when or before you grab the gun, GET OFF THE LINE OF ATTACK! Get out of the way of that bullet! Move your body to the side and forward toward the threat, enough to ensure that you don't get shot when the first round leaves the muzzle.

3 **Grab the gun.** Be sure to get a good grip on the gun. Use both hands if at all possible. You're going to use that death grip to keep the gun pointed at the attacker and/or away from innocents and yourself.

4 **Strip the grip.** Turn the handgun toward the attacker's thumb and away from his trigger finger (opening the gate), and stabilize the wrist. Yank the gun out of his hand. You can also turn the gun the opposite direction; it will just be harder to remove and there could be even more chance of firing the gun. Above all, make sure that you don't allow the gun to point at you or anyone else (except for the bad guy; you can point it at him!).

5 **Run away.** Even if you are fairly confident that you could operate the gun you just stole from your attacker, there are too many things to consider. Are you sure it's loaded? If not

77

he could attack again and then you'd be in trouble again. Is his weapon cleaned and properly maintained? If not, it could jam up and malfunction when you need it most. And are you absolutely sure you can operate that particular gun under stress? You won't have time to stop and think about it; you should know the gun before you attempt to use it. It's better to just train yourself to run away once you can do so safely. And take the gun with you.

Defensive Use of a Firearm

Whether using a handgun of any caliber, or a long gun – that is, a rifle or shotgun, the general use of a firearm is the same. The first rule of defensive use of any firearm is, do not pick up a firearm for use against another person unless you are genuinely concerned for your life or the life of another. In other words, do not shoot anyone unless you do so in defense of human life.

In training security officers in use of force guidelines, I always teach the same: deadly force is that force which a person uses, causing – or that a person knows or should know would create a substantial risk of causing – death or serious bodily harm. The use of deadly force is only permitted in situations in which there is a displayed capability, opportunity, and intent to kill or cause serious bodily harm to the officer or another human person. Deadly force does include the risk of not only death, but of serious bodily harm. In my training classes serious bodily harm is defined as injuries that create a substantial risk of death or that cause permanent disfigurement or prolonged loss or impairment of the function of any body part or organ. Some examples of serious bodily harm are paralysis, loss of a limb, loss of function of a limb, broken bones, head/neck/spinal injuries, serious cuts or burns, scarring, or serious disfigurement.

The reason I teach security officers this is because if they were to use deadly force against someone who, for instance, simply yelled at the officer without any indication that they intended to harm, the company could easily be sued for negligence and the officer could be charged and convicted of murder or manslaughter. The same rule applies for civilians. Even with "Stand Your Ground" and "Castle Doctrine" laws in place, self-defense is clearly outlined, and ends when the attacker retreats or becomes unable to attack. Restated, if your attacker runs away, it would be a bad idea to shoot him in the back.

Another point that should be made is that of targeting: where you should shoot someone if you have to do so. I hear many compassionate folks talk about shooting someone in the leg or foot, or even fantasizing that they will shoot the gun or knife out of the bad guy's hand. While any humanitarian on the planet would applaud the efforts of someone to save the evildoer's life by aiming at what they believe to be a nonlethal point, in actuality, it is far too difficult to perform in real life. The appendages of a human are small, fast moving targets, and when you miss (remember that your heart rate is going to be heightened due to survival stress), the bullet is going to end up somewhere beyond its target. In fact, it is very likely, especially with a high-velocity caliber such as a 9mm or .38 Special, or almost any rifle or shotgun round, that even if the bullet does hit a hand, arm, or leg that it will penetrate all the way through the target and end up on the other side, possibly striking a loved one.

The much better alternative is to aim center mass of the bad guy; shoot him in the upper torso, anywhere above the belly button. The reason for this being such a perfect target is that the torso is large and therefore is much easier to successfully shoot. Also, according to statistics derived from the Strasborg Tests in 1991, there is roughly a 60% chance of making contact with a rib when shooting at the torso of a person. That means that a bullet is more likely to stop within the body, and will do more damage. It isn't a guaranteed kill, and that's not our goal. Remember, we simply want to stop the attacker. A side note on shooting someone in the arm or leg: killing someone by severing the femoral or brachial artery with a bullet to the leg or arm is no better than the alternative. May as well make your shots count; aim center mass where you're a lot less likely to miss.

KNIVES

You've heard the old adage, "never bring a knife to a gunfight". But it's been my experience that it could be more foolish to bring a gun to a knife fight. Knives are very dangerous instruments in the hands of a trained user. And they can be just as dangerous being used by someone with absolutely no training.

The dangerous thing about a knife is, you don't have to aim it; just get within range and start cutting and/or stabbing. The wounds caused by even an accidental knife wound can be deadly, and you don't have to reload to continue cutting.

It's taught all over the country that when faced with a knife-wielding opponent, you need roughly 21 feet between you and the opponent in order to draw and fire a handgun in defense of your life. Why? Because it takes approximately 2 seconds for you to see a threat, recognize it as a deadly threat, decide to take action, draw your handgun, aim it, and pull the trigger. In two seconds a person 21 feet away can take off running and reach you before you ever get a shot off, even if you expect it. These stats are true to life; I've tried them over and over again. Now the bad news – at twenty-one feet you can fire at least one shot literally less than a second before your opponent reaches you; that's no guarantee that when you do shoot, your shot is on target! The fact that your opponent has reached you at all is almost a guarantee that he will cut you at least once, but there's no assurance that your bullet will find its target.

Now for some worse news – most fights involving a knife begin within arm's reach and end before the victim even realizes a knife was involved! Think about that for a second. The bad guy pulls a knife at close range and cuts you with it, but your adrenaline is already pumping and all you feel is what seems like punches to your lower torso. The attacker runs away and leaves you in a pool of your own blood…and then you realize what just happened.

If you find yourself at a knife's edge, its user demanding your money or property, give it to him. You can always get new stuff; you can't get a new you. But if they want more than just your stuff, put on your big-boy pants and get ready to fight.

Defense against a knife is very similar to defense against a handgun at close range. As I mentioned in the defense against a handgun, your attacker must be within arm's reach for this to work, so if he's standing just outside of arm's reach, threatening you with a knife, don't try to rush in and take the knife. It won't likely end well for you. Instead wait until he gets within range and then put the moves on him.

Defense against a knife

1 **Expect to be cut or stabbed.** The cruel reality is, a person who truly wants to kill you will not be as docile as some of the commercial self-defense videos depict. He will more likely rush in and stab several times in quick succession. He may slice with wide, arcing motions. Either way, you can safely assume that you will be wounded. Ignore that and fight through. Try to keep your wounds confined to non-vital areas, such as your outside forearms and shoulders. And understand that there will be blood involved – probably yours. Deal with it.

2 **Close the gap.** Again, you must be very close. Get in there, commit to the fight for your life, and overcome.

3 **Grab the weapon hand.** Whereas with a handgun you want to grab the gun itself, with a knife you just want to grab the whole arm because grabbing the knife will injure the tendons

SELF PROTECTION

and muscles in your hand and disable it. You're going to have to control the hand which holds the knife. Grab with both hands if at all possible. Grab with your whole arm if that's what it takes. Isolate the weapon hand and lock it down. Don't let it keep injuring you.

4 **Unbalance the attacker.** Break his balance down with a good shoulder butt or shove, trip him, or whatever takes his balance away and puts you in a position of power.

5 **Run away.** Don't try to get the knife away like you did the gun; he can't hurt you at long range with a knife. And no, throwing a knife at you isn't a realistic threat. Run away. Now.

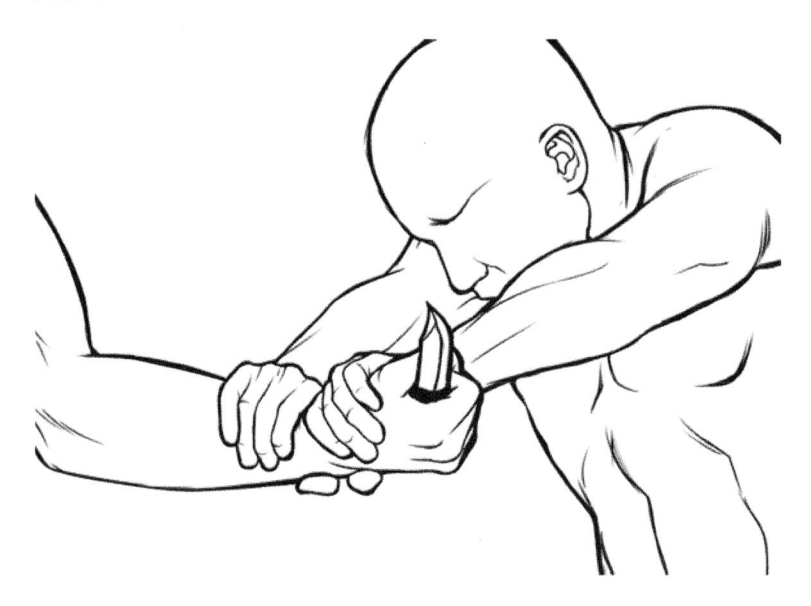

Defensive Use of a knife

If you happen to be the one with a knife in hand, facing someone who is trying to kill you, congratulations! You are now on the top of the food chain (unless there are more of them than there are of you). Now let's get you up to speed on how to use that thing to your advantage!

WEAPONS

1. **Full hand forward grip, weapon hand back.** Regardless of what certain "experts" will have you believe, keeping the knife semi-concealed along your forearm in a reverse ninja-grip will not make you any more lethal with a knife. In fact, it shortens your reach-out-and-touch-someone distance, and that's not a good thing. Furthermore, it makes it much easier for your attacker to control your arm, along with the knife. Let's not do that, shall we? Hold your knife in your hand the way you would hold a hammer; with a full-hand grip. Stand in a boxing or combat stance and place your defensive side forward, pulling your knife hand back. Keep the knife close to your center so you can control it and protect it.

2. **It is better to stab than to slash.** While slashing will obviously injure your opponent, stabbing is a more instinctive movement, and it is more efficient. Slashing relies on wide arcing movements which can more easily be grabbed or deflected, whereas stabbing usually takes the path of a straight line. Also, slashing techniques tend to fall short of their mark when the bad guy is wearing thick, heavy clothing. But stabbing with a long enough object will usually get through. And there are more objects with which you can stab someone, than there are with which you can slash. However, if a slash is what is available and natural to you at the time, then by all means, slash!

3. **Strike repeatedly until you are able to get away.** Don't stop with one stab or cut, no matter how injurious you believe it to be. If your attacker is still able to attack you, he is still a threat. The best thing to do is to stab repeatedly until your attacker is no longer attacking, but is retreating, and giving up.

STICKS

The use of blunt weapons to inflict damage has been a practice of individuals and military units for thousands of years. And somehow, with all our modern technology we just can't seem to put it down. Why? Well, because club-like objects are so good at causing blunt force trauma! And in your neck of the woods knives and guns may not be as readily available as they are here in Mississippi, but you can pick up nearly any blunt object and hit someone with it. Pick up a lamp, a glass bottle, broom or mop, or a host of other household items and you have a weapon.

Defense Against Club Type Weapons

Oftentimes, especially in crowds, an attacker will use a club type weapon from behind, striking his victim on the head. It is important to always know what's going on behind you.

If your attacker attacks from the front, or if you are able to place him in front of you ahead of time, here is how you can defend yourself against a club type weapon attack:

WEAPONS

1. **Expect to get hit.** Getting hit with sticks and clubs hurts a lot. Depending on where you get hit it can make you feel like immediately giving up. But don't give up, fight through the pain and survive.

2. **Close the gap.** Just like defending against the knife and the gun, you must close the gap and get in tight with the enemy. Don't step back when he starts swinging; all the force of a baseball bat or other club weapon as it is being swung will be in the last one-third of the weapon. You don't want to be on the receiving end of that, so get in closer to the opposite end. While there may be a good bit of energy at the end of the attacker's arms, it won't compare with the amount of force being created at the end of the stick.

3. **Grab the weapon hand(s).** Sure you could grab the weapon itself, but there's a lot of force being swung at you and there's a very real chance of breaking your hand. It's safer and more effective to grab the whole arm or even both arms if the attacker is swinging with both hands. Don't try to

block the weapon with a Karate style block; it will break your bones! You may have to absorb some impact from the swing, but if you followed step two, it will be all arm and no club.

4   **Circle out.** The weakest part of nearly any club weapon is the grip which the attacker has on it. If the weapon is long enough for you to grab, then do so. Using the same circle-out procedure to escape someone's grip on your wrist, apply some leverage close to the bad guy's grip and remove the weapon from him.

5   **Run away.** Don't stand there and attempt to use the frying pan against him; run away before he takes it back and uses it against you.

Defensive Use of a Club Type Weapon

It's pretty simple to use a club style weapon; hold on to it tightly and swing fast and hard. You may want to jab one end into your attacker and then follow up with a swing. Swing high, swing low, just keep swinging until you can safely escape and get help. Since you shouldn't be using a blunt object to bludgeon anyone to death unless your life is in imminent danger, you will want to maximize the efficiency of the weapon. In order to do that, you will want to strike your attacker in the head and neck area if possible. But really, if you are hitting him hard enough, almost anywhere will do.

The hardest part of using a club type weapon is identifying the objects which can be picked up and used on the spur of the moment when everything is happening so fast.

Her name was Rosemary. She was fun-loving, pretty, and streetwise. She was also the ex-girlfriend of a violent inmate in the detention facility in which I worked and she was staying with me for the weekend. He was out on bond and he decided to come say goodbye to her, since he was pretty sure he was headed to prison for a long, long time. I was asleep in my bed when I heard his drunken shouts. I went to the door just as he barged in. I instinctively punched him, knocking him off his feet, and then my fight-or-flight response decided it was time to run. I ran all the way through my apartment, past a handgun beside my bed, past a baseball bat behind the door, and past a pair of nunchakus hanging on the door knob. I passed up a tanto-blade knife hung on the wall as decoration, as well as a Samurai Katana and an English bastard sword in the living room corner before I realized that I had no reason to run. I turned to find him right behind me throwing a barrage of punches at my head. When the police arrived to arrest my assailant, the officer asked me, "Why didn't you pick up one of these weapons and use it?" The truth: it never occurred to me to stop and pick anything up. I just panicked.

By the way, what rule of protection did I violate that led to my assault that night? That's right, I didn't avoid dangerous people. Although Rosemary was not very dangerous, the company she kept was. That was a hard-learned lesson I won't soon forget.

CONCLUSION

The training officer stood before the newly hired security team and gathered his words. He had taught us in two weeks just about all he could about the technical aspects, the theories, and the protocols of protecting the military installation.

"There are bad people out there," he said. "When you come face to face with one of them, you'd better be ready. You can't wait until the moment arrives to decide how far you're willing to go. You've got to decide right now, before you go on post. Because if you wait until it's too late, you've already made your decision. And the bad guys already made their decision too." The captain was right. It was advice I'd never heard before, but it was good advice; advice I needed to hear. It was something we all needed to hear that day, and it's something you need to hear today.

The purpose of this book isn't to prepare you for war, or to indoctrinate you into the acceptance of violence, but to equip you with information which will help you avoid ever needing to use violence. Still, with all the avoidance and prevention and deterrence measures one can take there may one day come a time when the wolf comes knocking at your door. What you do in that moment is up to you. Will you defend yourself and your family at all costs, or will you turn the other cheek? Will the wolf emerge victorious, or will you? Think long and hard about that, because for good folks like you and me, killing another human being is not an easy thing to do, despite what you see in movies. But decide here and now, before you close this book, just what you are capable and willing to do. Because in the heat of battle is not the time to find out if you agree with your own conscience.

Take these truths which are chronicled within these pages and outline your own survival. I trust they will benefit you as they have me. I hope that peace finds you and follows you for all your life, and if you ever do find yourself staring into the eyes of the wolf, I hope you are prepared and able to survive.

> *"I am never proud to participate in violence, yet I know that each of us must care enough for ourselves that we can be ready and able to come to our own defense when and wherever needed."*

> — MAYA ANGELOU

Printed in Great Britain
by Amazon